The media's watching Vault!
Here's a sampling of our coverage.

VAULT
> the insider career network™

THE VAULT GUIDE TO
STARTING
YOUR OWN
BUSINESS

THE VAULT GUIDE TO
STARTING
YOUR OWN
BUSINESS

BY JONATHAN R. ASPATORE AND THE STAFF OF VAULT

Library of Congress CIP Data is available.

ISBN 1-58131-180-X

Printed in the United States of America

Table of Contents

Looking for a new challenge? The Vault Job Board has thousands
of top jobs for all experience levels. Visit www.vault.com.

VAULT CAREER LIBRARY

vii

Use the Internet's
MOST TARGETED
job search tools.

Vault Job Board

Target your search by industry, function, and experience level, and find the job openings that you want.

VaultMatch Resume Database

Vault takes match-making to the next level: post your resume and customize your search by industry, function, experience and more. We'll match job listings with your interests and criteria and e-mail them directly to your inbox.

Introduction

Everybody has a bit of entrepreneurial spirit in them – being an entrepreneur has nothing to do with age, gender, race or education. Not everybody chooses to tap this spirit though. Those who do give themselves the opportunity to create a type of success, wealth and satisfaction that can only be achieved by starting a business. This book will instill in you the confidence and knowledge to start your own business.

Having personally experienced the triumphs and difficulties of starting businesses, I can state confidently that being an entrepreneur is a way of life. You must believe in yourself, your ideas, and have the inner resources to go forward during difficult times. Starting your own business means becoming personally responsible for every facet of your company and taking on many roles. You must foster your belief in the future success of your company in each of your employees. You must believe in the future of your business and do whatever it takes for your company to succeed. In many cases, you must eat, sleep and breathe your business.

The purpose of the following chapters is to both help you begin thinking in an entrepreneurial manner, and to teach you the fundamentals of starting your own business. This book is meant to stimulate your mind and fan those glowing embers of entrepreneurial desire. Good luck, and start it up!

Looking for a new challenge? The Vault Job Board has thousands of top jobs for all experience levels. Visit www.vault.com.

VAULT CAREER LIBRARY

1

Entrepreneurial Thinking

CHAPTER 1

The entrepreneur's thought process

Entrepreneurial thinking is about recognizing opportunity and understanding how to capitalize on it. Entrepreneurs learn to see opportunity while others stick with what's out there. Learning how to think in an entrepreneurial way allows you to stay one step ahead of your competition, whether it be with your own business or with other aspects of your life. Everyone has a different perspective on what he or she would find useful. Learning to think like an entrepreneur means learning to use that unique perspective to improve or create products and services for others.

For example, you should remember those times when you find yourself wanting a product or service, only to find that it is not available to you. Or make a note if you think of a way to do something more efficiently. Look around and notice what people desire, or what you think they will want in the future. Remember that it can be just as profitable to improve upon an existing product or service as it can be to create an entirely new one.

The sheer number and diversity of people in this country and worldwide mean that there are multitudes of untapped markets. It just takes a little bit of creativity to reach them. Don't be afraid of ideas that seem odd or impractical – cars, computers and microwaves were all questioned or shunned at some point.

- What opportunities have you noticed that are not currently being exploited in the marketplace?

- What kinds of products or services have you always wished existed, but do not?

- What talents and knowledge do you have that will allow you to recognize opportunities in the marketplace?

Let your idea grow

If you feel that your idea has value and would make a positive impact in the marketplace, then create an environment in which it can flourish and grow; don't let the entrepreneurial thinking stop with you. Hire creative, open-

Looking for a new challenge? The Vault Job Board has thousands of top jobs for all experience levels. Visit www.vault.com.

VAULT CAREER LIBRARY

3

minded people and make sure they feel free to share their ideas. Look for people with the confidence to offer suggestions on ways to improve your business. Although entrepreneurs start with an idea or product, human capital is always their greatest asset.

Make sure your company organization is flexible. The path you expect your business to follow will probably change many times, as a result of new technology, marketplace changes or new ideas. Creative thinking can produce new ideas that change the course of your business; the ability of your business to efficiently and swiftly bring new ideas and products to the marketplace will mean the success or failure of your business. Remember that large companies often have a long lag time in bringing new products to market. As an entrepreneur, you should use this to your advantage and capitalize on your creative ideas in the timeliest manner.

Creative thinking has the power to take your business to new levels. Look at every aspect of your new business and assess what you could be doing in a more efficient way. Encourage creativity in your employees and give them voice to express their suggestions and ideas.

- How will your new business differentiate itself from its competitors?

- What are ways that your new business can use creative thinking to exploit available resources?

- How can creative thinking benefit your new business?

- How do you plan on looking for creative thinking in prospective employees?

- How will your business take advantage of the new ideas that your creative ideas produce?

Brainstorming

Once you've assembled a team of creative thinkers, make sure you tap their potential with frequent brainstorming sessions. These should involve time set aside for participants to throw out any ideas they come up with, no matter how nutty. No ideas should be criticized during the brainstorming session. After the session, participants can sort through the new ideas.

In many companies, brainstorming only happens when a problem presents itself. That's a missed opportunity. Set aside time at least once a month to brainstorm on ideas, not just solutions to problems, for your business. Brainstorm about new ideas for your existing business, possible partnerships, and tangents to your current line of business. The lifeblood of your business as an entrepreneur is new ideas; without brainstorming sessions, they may only present themselves haphazardly.

- What is the best environment for brainstorming?

- How can brainstorming help your company become more innovative and stay ahead of the competition?

- Which members of your business team would be good contributors to a brainstorming session?

A step ahead

Your business will always have some form of competition. When starting up it is important that you identify and study your competitors. Identifying the competitive advantages of your business will be critical to your success. Once you have entered the marketplace, your competitors may make changes in their businesses to counter your strategy. Therefore, it is important that your business remain a step ahead of the competition. Map out the future of your business, and where you and your competitors are heading – try to be first to bring a new product or service to the marketplace.

- Who are your competitors in the marketplace?

- What will your business offer that your competitors do not?

- What are the current goals of your competitors in the marketplace?

- How can you position your business to bring new products and services to the marketplace before your competitors?

- What industry trends will create new opportunities for your business in the future?

- How will you keep abreast of new developments at other companies to ensure that your business continues to offer a superior product or service?

Looking for a new challenge? The Vault Job Board has thousands of top jobs for all experience levels. Visit www.vault.com.

VAULT CAREER LIBRARY   5

The personal keys to entrepreneurship

Coming up with the actual business idea is the easy part of starting your own business. The real challenge of entrepreneurship is the process of building your business – an exhilarating and challenging process that forces you to understand and develop every segment of your company. While the following chapters will take you through the basics of getting your business established, you should remember that your personal vision and aspirations will be the foundation of your new business.

- What do you think are the keys to succeeding as an entrepreneur?

- How do you plan on achieving these goals?

Desire, persistence, confidence

First and foremost among your personal characteristics as a budding business owner, you must have the drive to succeed. You must envision your business succeeding. You must be willing to do whatever it takes to ensure success. You will probably have larger and more established competitors, but your desire to succeed will help you find advantages over them. You must also instill this desire in every one of your employees. Having a drive to succeed also means setting higher and higher goals. This keeps your company growing and excelling.

Dogged persistence is another must for the entrepreneur. Don't be discouraged if at first things don't work out. Try! Try again! You will inevitably encounter setbacks when starting a new venture. Many entrepreneurs have been rejected time and again, before going on to create extremely profitable businesses. You are bound to encounter many people who will discourage or ignore you. Move on and find the next person that will share your beliefs and passion.

Finally, you must exude confidence in your new business. Your confidence motivates others to invest, work for you, or become customers. You must be able to explain why your new business is going to be a success and convey this knowledge to others. Entrepreneurs often face rejection and criticism in starting their businesses. You must able to handle rejection and still remain confident in yourself, your abilities, and your ideas. Every person has a different set of tastes, opinions, and beliefs. Do not be discouraged by criticism. Instead, learn from others and seek out ways to appeal to a variety of personalities.

• What skills do you have that will help you capitalize on opportunities in the marketplace?

• Why is it that you want to start your own business?

People skills

The bonds you form with your contacts, employees, and customers will be the basis of your business. Think about the people that are most apt to believe in you and your new business – your friends and family. Why? You have established a bond of trust and respect with them and they believe in you. You want to establish the same sort of relationships with every one you know. Approaching potential customers, partners, or even investors with this understanding in mind is the first step to creating a solid relationship.

These relationships will also open new doors for you and your company. Gaining the reputation as someone good to do business with, or someone good to work for, is a sure formula for success. Always look to make additional business contacts and friends. The larger your circle of friends and business contacts, the more resources are available to your business.

Knowing the importance of personal bonds, the good entrepreneur never jeopardizes the reputation of his company by offering any product or service that does not meet or exceed his quality standards. Loyal consumers will result in repeat customers and good word of mouth – the best (and cheapest) form of advertising.

• What skills do you possess that will help you form relationships?

• What skills do you need to focus on to create the right image for your business?

• How can you make sure that others in your business employ the same people skills?

• What do you expect to learn from starting your own business?

• What skills do you need to develop to be an effective manager?

Building a network

Making contacts is an important part of building your new business and creating a web of resources for your company. Creating both personal and

Looking for a new challenge? The Vault Job Board has thousands of top jobs for all experience levels. Visit www.vault.com.

VAULT CAREER LIBRARY

7

professional bonds with other people will open doors for you and your company. Try to find common ground with your new acquaintances and make some sort of connection with them. Always have business cards on hand and use them as a way to casually exchange phone numbers. Follow up with these people as often as possible, whether by mentioning an article you read about the industry or by informing them of an upcoming event they may be interested in attending. Try to go to as many social and business functions as possible. Making contacts is crucial to the future success of your business.

Make a list of individuals that you would like to meet. Then determine your common interests. Think of every possible connection you could have with these people. Are your children at the same middle school? Do you belong to the same religious organization? Are you both golfers? Will they be attending an upcoming industry conference? Try to find the common link that will create a casual and relaxed first meeting. Once you do have the opportunity to meet, make a note of the place you met and the discussion you had. Pay attention to their interests and things that are important to them, whether they are business oriented or personal. It is appropriate to touch base with them or extend an invitation to some sort of gathering once every six months, just to keep the lines of communication open.

A good way to keep in touch with your industry contacts is to purchase a database program such as ACT or CardScan that allows you to keep updated files on contacts. These programs will also allow you to create notes on each individual and record your discussions. Creating a personal relationship with these individuals is the way to gain their trust and business. Even remembering something like the type of dog they have or the name of their child will make a great impression. Having similar interests and sharing common aspirations will also help to create a personal bond. Keeping in touch with people is the way to maintain professional and personal relationships and the best way to promote your business.

It's all about you

Starting your own business shifts responsibility squarely onto your shoulders. You will have the opportunity to create your ideal company and have a hand in every part of the operation. But, while running a startup is exciting, it is also a pitfall-laden process that necessitates attention to detail.

So why do it? Working for someone else means that you are always subject to the personnel decisions of that company. Starting your own business will put you in charge of your destiny and allow you to create your own schedules, agenda, and goals. You will also be responsible for every facet of your new business. This means you are now also responsible for every one else's performance and professional well being as well. On the other hand, you will be able to handpick your new employees and mold them to fulfill the vision you have for your company.

Enjoy what you are doing

Your new business must be something that you enjoy. You will be spending too much time on your new venture for it to be otherwise. If you truly enjoy what you are doing, your business will be more like play. Passion for your work gives you the confidence and perseverance to persevere amidst difficulties and setbacks. Find ways to make your new business enjoyable. Reward yourself for your hard work and small successes you achieve along the way.

Risks

Do not be afraid of the risks associated with starting a business. You encounter some amount of risk in everything you do, from crossing the street to putting your money in the stock market. Entrepreneurs are actually taking a well-controlled risk, because they are betting on themselves. If you start your own business, the company will live or die by what you do. Do not let others convince you of any extra risk associated with starting your own business. Risks are part of life; learning how to take calculated risks will ensure you make the proper decisions when starting your business.

Encourage employees at your company to take risks. Doing so will tap into their creativity and enhance their working performance. All of your employees have their own special talents and abilities; by giving them the ability to take risks, you maximize their performance. Reward those individuals who are taking smart risks, because they will be essential to the success of your business.

- What risks are associated with starting your business?

- How can you mitigate these risks by offsetting actions?

- How will you encourage your employees to come to you with new ideas and voice their opinions when they disagree with certain methods?

Looking for a new challenge? The Vault Job Board has thousands of top jobs for all experience levels. Visit www.vault.com.

VAULT CAREER LIBRARY   9

Planting seeds for future businesses

Whether you are ready to start your new business next week or next decade, you should always be planting the seeds for future businesses. Stay current with industry trends and advancements. Keep informed of developments in industries that interest you. Learn about the major competitors and the knowledgeable people in these industries. It is never too early to begin laying the foundation for future business endeavors.

- What people do you know who will be a valuable resource when you start your business?

- What publications will keep you abreast of the industries in which you want to start a business?

Now is the time

The marketplace is perpetually fluctuating; there is never truly an "optimal" time to start your business. But the sooner you start it up, the earlier you will gain control of your destiny. Naysayers can always come up with reasons why now is not a good time to start a business.

When an opportunity presents itself you must be ready to take advantage of it. The longer you wait, the more reasons you will find to postpone indefinitely. This does not mean you should quit your job immediately, but you should at least begin thinking in an entrepreneurial way and looking for opportunities to capitalize in the marketplace.

- What opportunity is it that you want to capitalize on?

- Why are you waiting to start your business?

- What individuals will be a valuable resource to your business?

- What events can you attend to make additional contacts and meet new people?

- How will you keep in touch with people who have the potential to help you in the future?

- What common preferences and goals do you share with these people?

- What individuals would it benefit you to become acquainted with?

Key Points

• You are in control of your destiny.

• Recognize opportunities in the marketplace.

• Always network.

• Risks will always be a part of life.

• There is no better time to start a business than today.

• Entrepreneurship is about people.

• The people who succeed the most are the ones with the desire and ambition, not the individuals with the most education.

Looking for a new challenge? The Vault Job Board has thousands
of top jobs for all experience levels. Visit www.vault.com.

VAULT CAREER LIBRARY   11

The Challenges of Starting a Business

"Putting out fires" is almost a daily task for entrepreneurs at any stage of their business. Entrepreneurs use innovation and creativity to find solutions where others see only roadblocks and problems. Businesses that succeed are ones that learn how to turn problems into competitive advantages for their company. For example, situations in which other businesses have run into trouble and retreated may represent excellent opportunities for your company to excel if you can find a way around these obstacles (and thus, find a comparative advantage).

The first ingredient required to excel in challenging situations is having the mindset discussed in the last chapter. Understand that you are going to have problems and face difficult situations daily, and look at them as a challenge for your business to establish an innovative and creative atmosphere.

- What do you anticipate will be the hardest part of starting your own business?

- How do you plan to overcome these difficulties?

- What will it take to make your business a success?

Time and resource commitment

Starting a business requires a commitment to success. This commitment means, primarily, time and money (and other resources). Whether you will be running your new business full or part time, it is crucial to plan the time and resources necessary to get your business going.

Start by mapping out estimated personal and financial costs and responsibilities. Make a list of everything you have to research, people you have to contact, and materials you need to get your business going. If you are currently employed, you still have responsibilities at your current job and you will not have as much time to spend on your future business. (This is how most businesses get started, so do not be frustrated by only having time during the evenings and on the weekends to devote to your startup.) Only by planning and using your time in a highly efficient manner will you understand when you are ready to open the doors to your new business full-time.

Many entrepreneurs fail due to poor planning and resource allocation. It is critical that you have a complete understanding of what it will take to get your business successfully started. Investors will not accept mediocre results, so it is crucial to be ready from the start. Proper planning will allow you to effectively manage your new company and focus on areas of growth, instead of overcoming inefficiencies and problems that could have been circumvented through adequate preparation.

If you are not planning on starting your business for a while, you can afford to spread out the planning over time. Still, it is never too early to begin planning for your business. Pick up and utilize pieces of information or contacts you encounter in the meantime.

- How much time do you currently have to devote to your new business?

- What resources will be required to start your business?

- How can you use your time in the most effective manner?

Financial planning

All businesses need financing, and your fledgling company is no exception. It's easy to underestimate the financial resources your business will require; hidden costs associated with starting a business are often almost impossible to imagine beforehand. A good way to begin financial planning is to analyze current competitor companies and their finances.

The most thorough, and best way to plan financing for your new business is by forecasting an estimated cash flow statement. With this statement, you should be able to determine the startup costs and the day-to-day operational costs of your business. The examples at the end of this book (in the sample business plan) will help you set up your estimated statement of cash flows. And when potential investors ask exactly how you will be using their investment dollars, you'll have a detailed analysis of projected costs to refer to.

Make a checklist of everything your business needs to get started. These may include employee benefits, insurance, uniforms, office supplies, merchant banking capabilities, incorporation, financial planning or industry research, just to mention the basics. Setting up a solid foundation now will alleviate future work. Take the time to think out the business structure so that you can focus on growing your business once it is up and running.

Running a startup means using resources creatively and avoiding unnecessary costs in the startup phase. Those costs represent money better spent on growing your business. Make sure to take advantage of available resources. Use your local copy center to bind reports and create signs and brochures, your local coffeeshop to meet with potential partners, employees, or investors, and your local library or the Internet to do research. Many magazines put their content online to be accessed by viewers for free. Save money by using your computer rather than buying subscriptions.

You can also cut hard costs when considering what will it take for you to attract others to come and work with you. During the start-up phase you probably won't be able to pay partners and employees huge sums of money, so you must find other incentives. The use of stock options and equity arrangements are excellent ways to attract employees without spending money up front. If the business takes off and does extremely well, they will be compensated with monetary and ownership rewards.

Even very successful startups encounter times when they do not have enough available cash to meet growth demands. Maybe there's an overwhelming response to their new product or service, or maybe unexpected costs have drained their cash. Try to have extra liquid (convertible into cash) assets on hand at all times.

You shouldn't stop once you've laid down your initial financial plan. After you have started your business, the marketplace will shift, altering your financial projections. Continually monitoring and understanding the necessary financing and cash flow required by your business will enable your new company to grow and prosper.

- What financial planning have you done to estimate costs?

- Are there comparable businesses in the marketplace that will help serve as a barometer?

- Have you put together an estimated balance sheet, income statement, and cash flow statement?

- Are there any tax issues involved with the type of business you are starting?

Looking for a new challenge? The Vault Job Board has thousands of top jobs for all experience levels. Visit www.vault.com.

VAULT CAREER LIBRARY   15

Your personal finances

If you are planning on leaving your job to run your new business full-time, it is especially important to map out how your personal finances will be affected. Determine if you can withstand a slow start to your new business. If you can, put money aside beforehand to live on until your business begins generating a steady stream of revenues. By analyzing your current financial situation you will be able to estimate the income you need to generate from your new business to maintain your current lifestyle. These estimates will be extremely important in determining the proper time to leave your job and focus full-time on your new endeavor.

Invest an amount of money in your new business that will still allow you to live in a suitable manner. Although being an entrepreneur may mean eating a lot of tuna, it shouldn't mean eating cat food. If you cannot afford to maintain a reasonable lifestyle, then you may want to seek financing from an alternate source. Although you may lose some of the equity of your new company, or have to pay interest on loans, you will have the peace of mind that comes from living comfortably. By taking calculated financial risks when starting your new company, you can hedge your losses if your business experiences difficulties, and allow yourself to continue the standard of living to which you are accustomed, even if the business fails.

- How much are you personally investing in your venture?

- What will you pay yourself once your business is started?

- With the money you have invested in your business, how long can you afford to operate at certain sales levels?

- What are the financial goals for your business?

- When do you expect your business to reach the break-even point?

Setting realistic goals

If financial planning is the backbone of a startup, goals are both the heart and head. Goals are what will keep your company constantly looking to improve, whether these goals be to find ways to operate more efficiently, create new partnerships, establish itself as the pre-eminent leader in its industry or make a snazzier web site. Goals provide both direction and drive.

At the same time, everyone in your company should be involved to some degree in outlining goals for your business. This involvement will shed light onto particular areas of your business that you may not have given much thought to. For example, if you are focusing on too wide a market, turn to your marketing director for advice. By letting your hired experts help set goals, you give your employees a sense of pride and your company an advantage.

As the leader of your new business, you must have the vision to understand tomorrow's marketplace today, and to set goals that will enable your business to capitalize on these developments. The most successful companies are run by people who have the foresight to understand the future of the marketplace. You should set reasonable goals, but do not hesitate to strike out into unchartered territory. This is how business legends begin.

- What is the goal of your business?

- How long before you expect to be making money?

- What is your projected start date for your business?

- Where do you want your business to be in six months, a year, and in five years?

- What individual goals do you have for yourself and any other employees?

Time management

Even if you are not planning to start your business full time for a while, it is important to schedule time to begin developing your venture, even if it's just an hour a week. If your venture is already up and running, it's a good idea to take a step back and re-evaluate the way in which you are spending your time.

Starting a business requires you to understand (and often perform) the jobs of every individual in your company. Because starting a business involves a plethora of tasks and minor crises, it is very easy to find yourself spending too much time on peripheral activities and not enough on growing your business. Dividing responsibilities is a critical part of managing your business and your employees. By giving the right people the right projects, you can both spend time on more valuable parts of your business and foster employee satisfaction. Remember that you are the nucleus of your company, and you should be spending your time on the most critical items.

Looking for a new challenge? The Vault Job Board has thousands of top jobs for all experience levels. Visit www.vault.com.

VAULT CAREER LIBRARY   **17**

There may be parts of your operation that you find too time consuming for both you and your employees. You should be willing to pay someone else (a contractor) to do these tasks. Understand what peripheral functions can be outsourced. Then you and your employees can spend time on more critical parts of your business.

- What responsibilities will you delegate in order to spend time on the core areas of your business?

- Are there certain tasks that are too time consuming and should be outsourced?

- How will you manage the growth of your business so you do not become overwhelmed?

The decision process

The decision to start your own business requires extensive research and planning. But do not be discouraged if your research and planning reveals that your idea would not be profitable or would be a poor fit for the current market. The ability to rebound from this conclusion and continue looking for new opportunities is one of the marks of a successful entrepreneur. Deciding to start your own business should be the result of conclusive research that shows your new business will be a success.

- Why is it that you want to start your own business?

- What research validates that your idea is a good one?

- What niche will your business fulfill in the marketplace?

Calculated risks

There are risks inherent with starting any business. There is always a chance that, due to unforeseen circumstances, your business will not succeed. The best thing to do? Hedge your bets. Take calculated risks to maximize the potential upside of entrepreneurship.

Taking calculated risks can mean a variety of things on different levels. On the most basic level, it can mean trying your buddy's computer before buying your own. On a higher level, it can mean forming a partnership with an existing company to use their equipment for a fee, instead of sinking precious capital into new machines before your business is on its feet. Taking unnecessary risks in the beginning stages of your business can cripple your company.

- What risks are associated with the type of business you are starting?

- How can you mitigate these risks with proper research and planning?

- What opportunities do you foresee in the future as having a major impact on your industry?

- Will the cash flow of your business support experimenting with new techniques and testing new waters?

The entrepreneur's leap of faith

Society has conditioned us to believe that job security means working for someone else. But the truth is that starting your own business is the only way to gain true job security. You are the boss, the one that makes hiring and firing decisions, the one personally responsible for the future of your company. You believe in yourself and your business. You have assumed full responsibility for your future.

If you are having difficulty making the leap of faith, try starting a business on a part-time basis. Maybe after tasting a bit of the excitement and the potential for true job security, you will choose to make that ultimate leap of faith and rely only on yourself for your future.

Starting a business can be very difficult and will result in many frustrations and joys along the way – sometimes, that frustration and joy will both come in the same minute. Maintain a positive attitude. Remember that building a company from scratch is not easy work: it requires innovation, time and persistence. Existing businesses do not want new competitors and will try to crush you. Focus on your passion for your business. Trust the cliché that entreats you to "look on the bright side." Learn from your mistakes and focus on your final goal.

- What do you find is the most frustrating aspect of starting your own business?

- What positives can you focus on throughout the difficult stages of starting your own business?

Looking for a new challenge? The Vault Job Board has thousands of top jobs for all experience levels. Visit www.vault.com.

VAULT CAREER LIBRARY

19

Key Points

- Attitude is everything.

- Believe in yourself and your idea – do not let others bring you down.

- Instill your attitude and belief into your employees.

- Building a successful business is never easy.

- Set goals for yourself, your company and each of your employees.

- Celebrate achievements.

- Always plan ahead.

- Never give up.

The Business Idea

CHAPTER 3

Many people build castles in the air. Few put foundations under them. Having an initial spark of inspiration is just the first step in the long process of developing a profitable business idea. An idea is like a prototype that must be tested under every possible condition. Your entrepreneurial thinking will yield many potential business ideas, but most won't hold up under close scrutiny. The reason the failure rate of startups is so high is that many entrepreneurs do not conduct the necessary painstaking research, analyzing timing, location, and both current and future market trends.

Your business idea need not be a completely new product or service. It can be a slight variation on what already exists in the marketplace. Startups can also flourish by sussing out existing great concepts that have been inefficiently managed and unable to reach the entire target market, and varying operations slightly to correct a competitor's mistakes. And huge markets such as long distance services, fashion & apparel, grocery stores, and movie theaters (just to name a few) require multiple businesses to handle the demands of their large customer bases. A startup may seek to carve out a niche in one of these large industries.

- What is your business idea?

- What other competitors currently exist in this industry?

- How does your business plan on making money?

Taking advantage of an opportunity

Like truffle-sniffing pigs, entrepreneurs are constantly hunting for opportunities others have passed over. Whenever you endure poor services, discover shoddy yet omnipresent products, or fail to find a product that you somehow desperately need, you've found an opportunity. Whether a variation of an existing product or service in the marketplace or an entirely new concept that will fill an aching void in people's lives, opportunities are all around us.

When you do experience an opportunity in the marketplace, be sure to take note of it. Always have a notepad or something else on which you can jot down your ideas. Ideas present themselves in the most unlikely of situations,

Looking for a new challenge? The Vault Job Board has thousands of top jobs for all experience levels. Visit www.vault.com.

VAULT CAREER LIBRARY 21

and you can't always rely on your porous head to retain all those eureka moments.

If you have already uncovered an opportunity, start your research! Through research, you'll discover if your idea is viable, and if anyone else has already thought of it. Opportunities exist everywhere in the marketplace, but some are not big enough on which to build a profitable business. Undoubtedly there's some market for vintage paperclips, but could you live on it? But if you feel that an idea may be successful in the future, make sure to record your thoughts and ideas so you can refer to them at a later stage. You never know when the market conditions may be right for your idea. Maybe someday the nation will be ready for eel burgers. By keeping an organized journal of your ideas and notes, you will be ready to tap potential ideas when the market is right.

Like the crocuses that flourish in spring, opportunities often present themselves for only a limited period of time. When you do spot an opportunity, seize it as quickly as you can, lest someone else do the same. Many large businesses cannot act swiftly because of the many levels of management and bureaucracy they must go through to head in a new direction. Use your flexibility to capitalize on opportunities in the marketplace before your competitors.

- How will you keep an accurate log of different observations and opportunities you witness in the marketplace?

- What will it take to capitalize on these opportunities?

- Why is it that other businesses are not doing this?

Identifying and assessing the opportunity

If you have an idea, determine whether it is viable. First, remember that you're not the only clever person in the world – try to figure out why other businesses have not successfully utilized your idea before. With this in mind, you can figure out what the comparative advantage of your business will be, how you will reach your target market where others may have failed, and how you will be able to bring your product or service into the marketplace. If going through this assessment convinces you that your idea will not hold up, don't get frustrated. Learning this now has saved you many headaches and lots of valuable time and cash.

- Why is it that other people have not executed your "great" idea?

- Do you possess additional skills, product knowledge, financing or contacts that allow you to succeed where others have failed?

Competitors

Even if no one has attempted precisely what you want to do, you will still have competition. The first web site devoted to dog training, though the first of its kind – already had competitors in books and manuals, private trainers and two-week obedience schools. But competitors can actually help you develop your business. Their presence will force you to constantly streamline your operations and develop new products and services. Know your competition: how they operate, what they provide, how they provide it and how you can do each one of these functions better. There must be a definable and positive difference between you and your business rivals. Sometimes it is enough to excel in just one area of the industry: if your pizza tastes iffy but is delivered in two minutes, you may have found a target market.

Studying the future of your industry and having experienced workers who understand the industry and consumer trends are essential to creating competitive advantages that will make your business profitable.

- What competitors currently exist in the marketplace?

- What are the strengths and weaknesses of your competitors?

- What reactions do you expect from your competitors when you enter the market?

- What resources give you a comparative advantage?

- What advantages and disadvantages do you have over your competitors?

- How will you crush your competition?

How big is it?

The size of the market that your business will try to reach is a vital consideration. Businesses can have widely disparate target market sizes: some specialize in a certain industry and cater to a segment of its population (for example, bridesmaid's dresses); others market their product or service to

Looking for a new challenge? The Vault Job Board has thousands
of top jobs for all experience levels. Visit www.vault.com.

VAULT CAREER LIBRARY   23

the widest possible audience (like orange juice). Although a larger market means more potential sales, aiming at the widest possible customer base isn't always the best strategy.

Make sure that there is a defined group of people that will be interested in your business. Get a sense of your market size through research at your local library. Find surveys and statistics that will be applicable to your business. Other businesses may also have published these sort of figures in their annual reports. You will need these numbers to calculate your estimated income sheet and statement of cash flows. Getting an accurate estimate of your potential market size is an essential part of predicting the profitability of your business.

- What is the potential size of your target market?

- What is the approximate revenue of this type of industry?

- What companies capture the largest percentages of market share?

- At what pace is your industry growing or declining?

- Have companies within your industry been growing or shrinking?

- Have there been a lot of new competitors entering the market?

Competitive advantage

The competitive advantages of your business are what give your company its edge. However, competitive advantages are transitory by nature. Industry leaders such as Chrysler, Microsoft, Barnes & Noble and Starbucks search continuously for new competitive advantages.

The competitive advantage of your business can be anything – a brand-new product or service, a clever or appealing variation on an existing product or service, a particular operating efficiency or maybe even a distinct marketplace image. Just look at the way coffeehouses like Starbucks have revolutionized the coffee industry. Coffee is just a bitter drink made from roasted beans, but add to that hot (or iced) java a casual setting, great music and a variety of flavors, and you've got a recipe for success. Even packaging can jazz up otherwise mundane foods, products, and services. Why do you think cereal boxes are always changing?

- What is the competitive advantage of your business?

- How will you compensate when other competitors emerge?

Profitability

Certain businesses yield greater profit margins than others, but profit margins do not have to be very high for a business to make money. With high turnover and limited inventory, you can still make a great deal of money. The key is determining a fair market price for your product or service that provides the customer with an incentive to buy and still allows you to make money.

Sometimes it takes years for companies to become profitable. Due to initial expenses and growth costs, even a very popular business may not be profitable. Laying the proper foundation for a growing company costs money and may mean you will lose money for years. But don't prevent yourself from spending money on products and services that will make your company more successful in the future just to be able to say you turned a profit. Usually these items pay for themselves and result in huge dividends at a later time. Part of good entrepreneurship is knowing when to invest in the appropriate resources to help your company grow. Well-known companies such as America Online and Cablevision only became profitable after years of spending money to fuel growth, market share and name recognition.

- What do you anticipate the profit margins of your business to be?

- What are the largest variables that affect these numbers?

- What will it take to improve your profit margins?

- How long do you anticipate before your business will be profitable?

- What tax methods will help you accurately estimate the financial situation of your business?

Take a good look

It is essential to have your business idea evaluated from many different perspectives – others will be able to see different strengths and weaknesses in your proposed business than the ones you saw. The wider the range of feedback, the better. Make sure that in addition to focusing on the comments of your target market, you introduce your idea to a cross section of people.

Say you are trying to start a store that carries a special line of sporting clothes for women. You would want to speak retail store owners. But you would also want to interview other women who have some interest in becoming more physically active, and men who buy gifts for women.

Looking for a new challenge? The Vault Job Board has thousands
of top jobs for all experience levels. Visit www.vault.com.

VAULT CAREER LIBRARY   **25**

Remember, while specialization can be very profitable if the market segment chosen is largely untapped, the larger your market, the higher the potential sales. Getting feedback from all different types of people will help you to see your business in a whole new light – the feedback can lead to adjustments that make your business appeal to a larger audience than you were initially targeting.

In seeking a range of perspectives on your idea, you might consider doing a small-scale "trial run" of your product or service. This need not be an intense study of the focus group and double-sided-mirror type. Your family and friends make excellent guinea pigs. The government-funded Small Business Administration (SBA) offers free help to entrepreneurs in most areas of the country. They will help you with your business plan and provide consulting from their small business advisors. Use the SBA and put those tax dollars to use! Suck the marrow out of every possible resource you have. While briefing others on your idea, you may even find a few interested investors, partners, employees, or customers along the way.

If you're asking for opinions, don't get frustrated by negative feedback. Although positive comments are great for your confidence, they will not necessarily help your business. Constructive criticism is what indicates weaknesses and areas of untapped potential.

- What are the best sources of feedback for your business idea?

- What evaluation techniques will you use to make your product or service appeal to the largest group of people possible?

- What ways are there to evaluate your competitors in the marketplace?

- How will you evaluate your own business on a regular basis to improve in certain areas?

- Have you established a network of outside advisors to assist you in your business?

- What constructive feedback have you received that will benefit your business?

Company goals, personal goals

Establishing goals for your business is a constant process that is essential to transforming an idea into a successful business: they give you and your employees something to focus your efforts on. Goals should be re-evaluated regularly, at least every few months.

Of course, you should tell your employees about these goals. But in addition to company goals, each employee should have his or her own personal goals. Encourage employees to come up with their own objectives; meet with them to discuss them. This is a great opportunity to establish relationships with your employees and understand what they do on a daily basis. During these sessions, you should examine how well they have done in reaching their previous goals.

Many business owners re-evaluate their goals on a daily basis. The first thing they do every day is establish their daily goals, and re-evaluate their short-term (generally three months) and long-term (generally one year) goals. Starting a business requires an incredible amount of work. It's easy to become distracted from what you need to be doing for your business to succeed.

- What is the goal of your company?

- What are your short-term, medium, and extended goals?

- What goals do your employees have individually?

- How will you reward individuals who are successful in reaching their goals?

Calculated risks

Taking calculated risks when implementing your idea helps protect your business. Plan for every possible scenario. A certain amount of risk is involved in every business decision, but learning how to regulate these risks will ensure a limited downside.

Major corporations have entire departments devoted to regulated the company's risk. Investment banks, for example, "hedge" their positions so downturns in their investments are counterbalanced by upswings in other holdings. Look over the areas of your business that you feel may be exposed to more risk than others.

Looking for a new challenge? The Vault Job Board has thousands
of top jobs for all experience levels. Visit www.vault.com.

VAULT CAREER LIBRARY   27

- What risks are associated with the type of business you are in?

- How can you effectively manage your business to avoid being overexposed to these risks?

Flexibility

As marketplace trends continuously change, your company must be able to provide new products and services that meet the fluctuating desires and preferences of each individual – you must be willing to alter and evolve your business idea.

Having a small business means that you will not have all of the resources your larger competitors will have. Therefore, you will have to compensate by creating a niche for your business within the marketplace. Being flexible to new ideas and able to change course will allow your business to test a variety of strategies that larger businesses do not have the luxury to experiment with. Also, as a small business you should be able to move more quickly to get a product to market than those memo-laden, bureaucratic giants.

When you do choose a new plan of action, make sure to update your short-and-long-term goals for your company. Innovation and flexibility will allow your business to be the first one to capitalize on new opportunities within the marketplace.

- What innovative resources will your business have available?

- How will your business use innovation to develop improvements to your products and services?

- As your company grows, how will you remain flexible to be able to experiment with new ideas?

Image

Having the right image will give your company increased value in the eyes of your customers   Every experience your customer has with any aspect of your business will affect your image. The design of the logo, the name of your company and even the way you answer the phone will shape the way customers view your business.

The name of your business should be succinct and make a lasting impression. Any sort of slogan or description of your business should be brief and appealing to your target audience. Get professional business cards that give people a number of ways to get in touch with you (phone number, fax number, e-mail, beeper, and web address). Give your employees titles that reward them with feelings of importance; they'll be more invested in the company and will project an enthusiastic image. Participate in community service programs to project a sense of caring.

Even though your business may be small, there are ways to create an image that is literally larger than life. Shine a spotlight on any partnerships or joint ventures your business has with identifiable companies in the marketplace. If you are working with people in different locations, show that you have a presence in different regions, thus making your company appear more substantial. Produce a Web site for your company that explains your business and offers your customers the option of purchasing your product or service online – media and technology have the ability to transmute a small-time operation into a something much larger in the eyes of the viewer. Print hats, coffee cups, and T-shirts to give to both employees and customers. Although your business may be small, a larger-than-life image can help it grow to the next level.

- What do you want the image of your business to be?

- What image will your target market most readily identify with?

- What will be the reason consumers choose your product or service over others in the marketplace?

- How can you project and improve the image of your business?

Partnerships and joint ventures

Partnerships and joint ventures are fast becoming the way for small businesses to move to the next level. As consolidation occurs in many industries, many smaller companies are clinging to the coattails of larger companies. Joining forces with a well-known company gives your business instant credibility and a great springboard.

It is important to realize that partnerships often begin with personal relationships; people want to do business with those they know and trust. Find businesses that complement yours and try to establish working relationships with them. Go to industry shows, schmoozy conferences and parties, and any other place where you will have a chance to meet people.

Looking for a new challenge? The Vault Job Board has thousands of top jobs for all experience levels. Visit www.vault.com.

VAULT CAREER LIBRARY   29

Find out what individuals your friends can put you in touch with. It takes time to build a relationship that gives you an opportunity to establish a partnership. Get to know that person on a personal level before you jump into suggesting partnership ideas. Take them out to breakfast or lunch to discuss what is going on with their business. Even if you are not able to form a partnership, this person may refer you to individuals who may want your product or service.

At the same time, you must realize that even with a personal connection, you need to have something that will make a partnership worthwhile. As a small company, you will often have to give up more in order to form a partnership with a better-known company. While there are many different ways to form partnerships – dual promotions, joint products, licensing – even partnerships formed on the simplest level can have a valuable impact on your business. Offer the brochures of another company in your stores. Put a link to their web site on yours. Even a small partnership effort will create the opportunity for bigger things down the road.

- What companies have interests that are compatible with the products and services of your business?

- What major industry players would you benefit from having a partnership with?

- What can you offer these companies in order to entice them to engage in a partnership with your business?

- How do they stand to benefit from a partnership with you?

- What contacts and resources will help in making contact with potential companies to form partnerships?

- How can you increase your base of contacts?

Future plans

Even before you start your business, you should have an idea what you want to get out of it. Admittedly, it's tough to think about this when you're just starting out. Yet it is always important to envision what you see as the future of your business.

Every person has different reasons for starting a business, but the one common reason is to make money. Entrepreneurs make the majority of their money when they sell their business or take their company public.

If you are seeking investors, they will want to know how they are going to get their investment back. Whether you buy them out, sell the company or do a stock offering, investors want to know what their outcome will be. Having plans for your business will help give you future direction and attract investors.

Understanding when it may be time to sell your business or move on to something else is another important part of successfully implementing your idea. If opportunity for expanding is dwindling and there is a premium on your business, it may be time to think about selling, even if you could find other ways for your business to offer new products and services. Entrepreneurial thinking is about capitalizing on opportunities in the market. If someone is offering to buy your company for a high price, you should probably sell. There are endless opportunities available out there – once you have the experience of starting a business, it becomes a lot easier to start another one.

- What do you envision as the future of your business?

- How do you plan to build your company to accommodate these plans?

- What will it take to grow your business to the next level?

- What industry developments will play a large part in shaping the future of the marketplace?

- Is this something that you see yourself running for a long time or do you hope to cash out at a later stage when the company is profitable?

Key Points

- The idea is the easy part. Implementation is the hard part.

- There are many good ideas waiting for someone to take advantage of them, but figure out why no one has succeeded with your idea.

- Thoroughly research your idea before you begin implementation.

- Conduct trial runs of your ideas. Take your business idea and mold a public image out of it.

Looking for a new challenge? The Vault Job Board has thousands
of top jobs for all experience levels. Visit www.vault.com.

VAULT CAREER LIBRARY   31

• Form partnerships with other companies.

• Know the end goal of your business idea – and don't be afraid to reach it by selling your company

• Set company goals and encourage your employees to set individual goals.

The Business Plan

CHAPTER 4

The business plan is an essential element of starting any business. It puts all of your ideas and research into one organized report that explains the nature of your business. No matter how basic and straightforward your idea is, you should always write a business plan. Writing a plan actually generates new ideas and forces you to flesh out current ones. A plan creates structure and organizes your thoughts; it should include the main strategy and research you have accumulated. The plan will serve as an operating manual when you start your business.

In this chapter, we will follow a business plan from start to completion. At the end of each section there will be an example of how each section could be developed. (There is also a complete business plan in the Appendix section at the end of this book.) Although every business plan is different in content and style, these samples will help you to begin generating your own ideas. The best way to learn how to write your own business plan is to read and understand others.

You will show others your business plan to generate feedback and interest in your concept. Investors, loan officers and potential partners will always ask to see a business plan so they can get a comprehensive understanding of your venture and vision. Not only should the plan give detailed financial information, but it should be a creative presentation that captivates the reader. It should read like a story that builds excitement and makes them want to become involved. The business plan is the tale of how your company will become a success.

General tips

Remember the discussion of company image in the last chapter? Generating a polished business plan package is an important initial step in creating a positive company image. If financing is necessary to start your venture, the business plan is the most important document in the eyes of the potential investor. Therefore, you should take care that your business plan is professional in tone and appearance.

Every page of your business plan should include your company name and contact information. Use a consistent format throughout the plan that makes

Looking for a new challenge? The Vault Job Board has thousands of top jobs for all experience levels. Visit www.vault.com.

VAULT CAREER LIBRARY   33

it easy for the reader to navigate between different sections. Make sure to double-check spelling, grammar and punctuation throughout the document. Have others read it over. Include reference articles and other pieces of information that support your ideas. Use graphics throughout your plan to spice up the presentation. When you have finished, have copies of your business plan printed and bound.

Your business plan does not have to be long, but it must include all of the information necessary to give your reader a comprehensive understanding of your business. Potential investors want to see that you have investigated and researched your idea and understand what it will take to succeed. Stress the comparative advantages of your business and how you will use these to leverage your company. It is also important to emphasize the resources and skills that you bring to the table. This is a chance for you to explain why your business will make it and what amount of money and time it will take to achieve the goal.

Writing a business plan will also force you to express your ideas in a more concrete form. Speak with other business owners, consult with experts on entrepreneurship and contact your local Small Business Administration office to get help from people familiar with the process.

Cover & introductory pages

The cover page of your business plan should bear the name of your company, the logo, and contact information. The introductory page should include your name as the owner of the business and a very brief (two or three sentence) description of your business. Don't try to do too much with your cover and introduction pages. These pages are simply meant to encourage the reader to keep going.

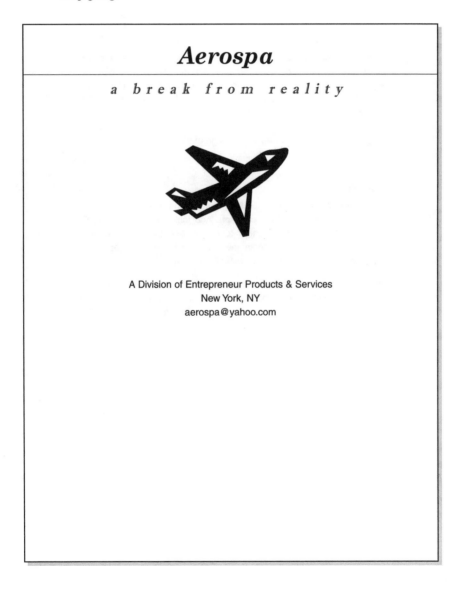

Aerospa

a   b r e a k   f r o m   r e a l i t y

A Division of Entrepreneur Products & Services
New York, NY
aerospa@yahoo.com

Looking for a new challenge? The Vault Job Board has thousands
of top jobs for all experience levels. Visit www.vault.com.

VAULT CAREER LIBRARY   **35**

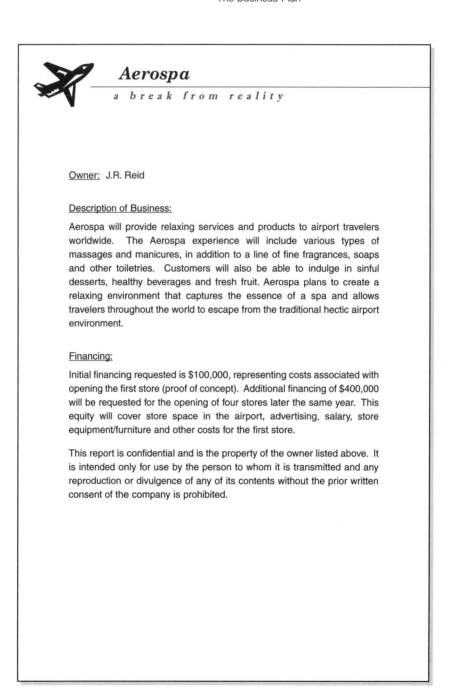

Aerospa

a break from reality

Owner: J.R. Reid

Description of Business:

Aerospa will provide relaxing services and products to airport travelers worldwide. The Aerospa experience will include various types of massages and manicures, in addition to a line of fine fragrances, soaps and other toiletries. Customers will also be able to indulge in sinful desserts, healthy beverages and fresh fruit. Aerospa plans to create a relaxing environment that captures the essence of a spa and allows travelers throughout the world to escape from the traditional hectic airport environment.

Financing:

Initial financing requested is $100,000, representing costs associated with opening the first store (proof of concept). Additional financing of $400,000 will be requested for the opening of four stores later the same year. This equity will cover store space in the airport, advertising, salary, store equipment/furniture and other costs for the first store.

This report is confidential and is the property of the owner listed above. It is intended only for use by the person to whom it is transmitted and any reproduction or divulgence of any of its contents without the prior written consent of the company is prohibited.

Executive summary

The executive summary portion of your business plan should give the reader an in-depth understanding of how your business will operate. It is a snapshot of your entire business plan and gives the reader a framework to understand your idea. This section is generally no more than a couple of pages in length and is written after completing the business plan. The executive summary is usually written last because you want to be able to look through the rest of the plan and summarize the key points.

Although the cover and introductory pages should grab the reader's attention, the executive summary is the real "teaser" part of your business plan. This is your chance to get readers excited about your potential business and demonstrate to them how you are going to succeed. Sometimes, venture capital firms and other investors will read only this section to determine if they are interested. Consequently, it is imperative that you grab the attention of the reader and immediately convince him or her of the merit of your idea.

Looking for a new challenge? The Vault Job Board has thousands
of top jobs for all experience levels. Visit www.vault.com.

VAULT CAREER LIBRARY   37

Aerospa

a break from reality

Executive Summary

Aerospa is designed to be a place where travelers can escape from the stress associated with airline travel. Millions of people travel through airports daily, creating an available and immediate audience. Most people arrive early for flights and are forced to wait. Others are delayed by the constant problems associated with airports. These people currently go to a bar or restaurant in the airport or wait at their gate. There exists no public place where travelers can go to relax and escape from the stressful environment common in airports. Aerospa will fill this void in airport travelers' lives by offering an affordable escape. Aerospa will be able to help every person relax during their visit. Aerospa will have a plush, modern interior, a welcome change from the gloomy decor of most airport stores and restaurants, further enhancing the Aerospa experience.

Aerospa will offer the following services to help our customers feel better and relax: manicures, 10-and 20-minute neck, back and head massages, and "cool-downs/warm-ups" where customers can indulge in cooling/heating packs placed strategically on their bodies to soothe sore muscles. Future additions may include facials, pedicures, tanning booths, face wraps, foot massages and full body massages. While receiving any treatment, they can plug into headphones and listen to their favorite music. Also being considered is the possibility of offering customers fabulous desserts and healthy fruit drinks. Aerospa will carry high-end facial and body products, which will be marketed as both great gift items and personal treats.

Airports are unique because of the advantage of having a captive audience. Travelers are accustomed to dealing with lousy food, terrible service and an uncomfortable atmosphere when going to airports. By offering a distinctly different environment in an uncomfortable atmosphere, men, women and children will all flock to Aerospa. Spas can be opened in airports worldwide and multiple locations can be opened in larger airports.

Aerospa

a break from reality

Executive Summary, cont'd

Beauty salons and massage parlors exist all over the world. However, nothing of the sort currently exists in airports, let alone a combination of the two. We are proposing a simplified version of the products and services spas offer. We wish to offer only a select set of services that are convenient to our customers. They can drop their bags at the door and indulge in a manicure or massage while listening to soothing music or reading their favorite magazine.

The financing needed for this venture includes the start-up funds necessary to open the first store, followed by future financing to open an additional four stores in the first year of business. Once these stores are opened, they will fuel future growth for Aerospa airport locations nationwide. Funding will provide for rental space, interior decorating, store equipment, personnel and other associated start-up costs. Aerospa plans to expand rapidly to other national and international airports.

Looking for a new challenge? The Vault Job Board has thousands
of top jobs for all experience levels. Visit www.vault.com.

VAULT CAREER LIBRARY   39

Industry analysis

The market information/industry analysis section of your business plan should include all relevant information on competitors and possible outside influences that will affect your business. In order to put this section together, it is important that you study your competitors and experiment with their products and services. Determine past events that have brought the industry to its current form. Understand what future developments will be important to the landscape of the industry. Investigate developments and changes in the industry you can capitalize on. Speak with your friends, co-workers and fellow business owners to get an understanding of the marketplace, then report your findings in the business plan.

Market research done to help you focus on enhancing your comparative advantage in the marketplace can be used in a business plan to show that you've "done your homework."

Aerospa

a break from reality

Industry Analysis

Airports are valuable space to reach customers through advertising, vending units, and storefronts. Airports create their own captive markets where consumers are forced to pay premiums for products and services.

Massage parlors and beauty salons have long been popular in the United States. There are a wide variety of salons and spas, from the extremely upscale to the mundane. Millions of people get manicures and receive massages weekly. Aerospa will only offer limited services that are targeted to airport travelers. Others treat themselves to some spa treatment at the end of a stressful day or when they have extra time on their hands.

Stress has been proven to be a cause of mental and health problems worldwide. As the hours people work continue to increase and on-the-job travel becomes routine, stress will continue to rise in the workplace, home and other areas. Aerospa offers a way for travelers to relax in a comfortable environment.

Description of venture

The description of venture section is a detailed analysis of your company. Where the executive summary is only a page or two that briefly outlines your business idea, the description of venture is meant to be a comprehensive explanation of your company. Give the reader an accurate understanding of what your business is about. Share your future goals and vision for the company. Describe the personal skills, resources and contacts you have that will make your business a success. Describe how you came upon the idea and what makes it different from what already exists in the marketplace.

In this section, you should provide thorough research on the industry and your competitors. Give detailed explanations of how your competitors are conducting business, highlighting their strengths and weaknesses. Web sites such as Dun & Bradstreet (www.dnb.com) and Vault (www.vault.com) are excellent sources to find out about comparable companies in the marketplace. Explain how you will exploit the weaknesses of your competitors. In this section, the reader should learn exactly how you are going to make your business a success. Even if you have the cleverest idea in the world, if you do not have proper operational and managerial methods your new business will wither on the vine.

- What is the product or service you are offering?

- Why will people buy this product or service?

- What resources will you need to start your business?

- How are potential customers going to find out about your business?

- What industry analysis makes you think your business will be a success?

- How do you plan to sell the product or service?

- What additional resources will be required to run your business?

- When do you plan on starting your business?

- Where will your business be located?

- How do you plan to manage your business?

- What future developments can enhance your business?

- What are your long-term goals for your business?

Looking for a new challenge? The Vault Job Board has thousands
of top jobs for all experience levels. Visit www.vault.com.

VAULT CAREER LIBRARY   41

Aerospa

a break from reality

Description of Venture

Aerospa plans to open five stores in different airports in its first year. We plan to open 10 stores the second year and 25 the third year, including an international store and multiple locations in major airports. Our ultimate goal is to open an Aerospa in every major airport worldwide. Once the first Aerospa is established, it will be easy to replicate and adapt the model to any location. We will also be able to obtain more favorable contracts in prime airport locations.

Each store opened will require renovation and training for new staff members. The bulk of the expenses will be for renovation, equipment and furniture and leasing the storefront. Once these expenses have been incurred there will be minimal monthly costs associated with upkeep of the store.

Approximately two shifts of five employees throughout the day will be needed. If the store is inundated with customers, additional room will be created to hire more staff. Each store will be open between 8 AM and 7 PM, with staff being present 30 minutes before and after hours of business, with an hour for lunch. There will be four trained professionals that will be able to administer both massages and manicures. The manager will be required to oversee operations, run the cash register and check baggage.

The following represents a possible list of products and services offered in Aerospa stores:

The Aerospa Experience

Manicures $12
Massages Neck and Back 10 Minutes $16
Massages Neck and Back 20 Minutes $ 29
Scalp add $5
Cool Down add $ 5
Heat add $ 5

Aerospa

a break from reality

Description of Venture, cont'd

Aerospa Aromatherapy

Aromatherapy Candles
Skin Lotions
Bath Gels
Heating and Cooling Packs
Massage Rollers

Aerospa Indulgence

Natural Fruit Juices/Shakes
Deserts
Ice Creams and Sorbets

Prices are comparable to local city prices.

The secret of Aerospa is its ability to generate profits and revenues very quickly once initial expenses have been covered. After the initial expenses associated with opening the store are incurred, there are relatively few monthly costs and almost every service offered produces 100% profit (minus rent and labor). In addition to the initial basic products and services being offered, there exist many other profitable opportunities for Aerospa including facial, hair and body products, aromatherapy gifts, gift certificates, commercial in-store advertising and possible expansion into commercial office buildings. Aerospa will succeed because of the products and services offered to a captive audience and its ability to reproduce its winning formula for profitability in airports worldwide. Long-term goals include franchising and a public stock offering.

Looking for a new challenge? The Vault Job Board has thousands
of top jobs for all experience levels. Visit www.vault.com.

VAULT CAREER LIBRARY   43

Operation/production methods

The more efficiently your business can get its product or service to the market, the higher your profit margins. The operation/production section of your business plan should give the reader a general understanding of how you will create your product or administer your service in the marketplace.

Depending on the type of business you are starting, there are different costs associated with bringing your products or services to customers. For example, the advent of the Web allows individuals to create a storefront online, without having to pay for rent or salespeople. This method has brought to life thousands of new companies that are taking advantage of this new, cheap, effective way to bring their product or service to the marketplace. This is just one example of how an operational method may have a drastic effect on every business. Using the correct number of employees and hiring people with specific skills is another essential aspect to maximizing your resources.

Explain how your business will use both creative and mundane ways to cut costs.

- Will your business be manufacturing a product or providing a service?

- How will you bring this product or service to the marketplace?

- How will you reach your target market?

- What additional resources will you need?

- Who will be responsible for the various stages of production?

- Where will you get your equipment, supplies or merchandise?

- How will you store these items?

- How will you establish an effective inventory control system?

Marketing

The marketing section of your business plan should explain how you plan to get the word out about your business and the type of image you are trying to create. Even if you are offering the best product or service since chocolate-covered cherries, you will never make a dime if no one knows about it.

Building the right image for your business is a critical part of the buzz you want to create about your product or service. There are many different ways of reaching customers: word-of-mouth, the media, paid advertising and the Web. We will review these in a later chapter, but for now, understand that discussing these strategies in your plan is an important part of convincing potential investors that you have thought through your business idea.

Partnerships and joint ventures lend credibility to your business. When an enterprise is in the beginning stages, being able to show relationships with other companies in the marketplace makes it more attractive to readers. This section is the place to note such partnerships.

- Why would people want to use your product or service?

- What is your target market?

- What are the most effective advertising media to reach your target market?

- What image are you trying to create for your business?

- What partnerships can you use to leverage your image?

- What contacts and resources are available to you in getting special deals on advertising rates?

Looking for a new challenge? The Vault Job Board has thousands
of top jobs for all experience levels. Visit www.vault.com.

VAULT CAREER LIBRARY   **45**

Aerospa

a break from reality

Merchandising Plan

The physical store will have an area where the four specialists will be able to give massages and manicures. There will be an area in the back where people who have received manicures may go to dry their nails. While drying their nails they can listen to music or read magazines. The register will be in the front along with chairs for customers waiting in line. Behind the register will be an area for customers to store their bags and luggage. The design for the store will be subcontracted to a construction company that can create the best image in our stores while complying with airport regulations.

Facial and aromatic merchandise will be purchased from several respectable manufacturers. Items such as soaps, shampoos, candles, powders, bath gels and lotion will be available for sale. In addition, customers will be able to purchase packs of multiple massages or manicures to give in gift certificate form to friends and family who are also business or vacation travelers. Customers will also be able to order gift certificates via our web site and have them mailed to travelers coming to visit them.

Magazines and newspapers will be available for reading while customers are receiving massages and manicures. Customers will also be able to listen to a wide variety of CDs while receiving services and watching television.

Aerospa

a   b r e a k   f r o m   r e a l i t y

Marketing Plan

Aerospa plans to market its services through media such as airline magazines, in-flight programming, airport billboards, network televisions in airports and other airport advertising space. Aerospa will market itself in public places with heavy traffic flow. We have already established a partnership with a major TV network. The network will provide our TVs in return for our guarantee that half our televisions be tuned to the network.

The strength of Aerospa is that it can provide a service to customers that is almost 100 precent profit in a brief period of time while having little to no inventory. It will be important to design the layout of the store to provide ways for people to enter and exit the store without feeling crowded. The solution to this may be to erect a wall in between the waiting area and where the massages and manicures are being performed, to further differentiate the separation between the airport and Aerospa. We will also offer gift certificates and sampler packs. These will serve as ideal housewarming and thank-you gifts. We will also do this with our facial and aromatherapy products. In addition, we will offer customers a discounted rate when they buy a book of five manicures or massages. Customers wishing to order gift certificates or products will be able to do so via our web site.

Aerospa will create a cozy and plush atmosphere with lighting, plush furniture, mirrors, track lighting and pleasant scents (incense or potpourri). Aerospa will also rely heavily on comment cards from consumers to help us make alterations and additions to our products and services making the "Aerospa experience" even more enjoyable.

Looking for a new challenge? The Vault Job Board has thousands
of top jobs for all experience levels. Visit www.vault.com.

VAULT CAREER LIBRARY   47

Organizational structure

Your plan must include a description of the company's organizational structure. This includes yourself, your employees, the board of directors, and any outside advisors. Each of these people plays an important role in the success of your business, so potential investors will want to know about them.

The board of directors is the advisory group that will oversee your business. Directors with industry experience, contacts, and who are familiar with your type of business will prove to be valuable resources to help shape and grow your company. As with joint ventures and partnerships, well-recognized members of your board should be played up in your business plan to establish credibility.

Outside advisors are people who are not formally connected with your company, but who provide advice and suggestions for your business. As with your board of directors, these advisors can lend credibility to your venture. Most young entrepreneurs try to find older, more established individuals (professors, high-level execs, etc.) as advisors.

Although planning your organizational structure from the beginning will help you handle growth and define the roles of each individual within your company, understand that this structure must be able to adapt and expand as the company grows. This understanding of the importance of an evolving organizational structure should also be conveyed in the business plan.

- Who will initially be part of your business team?

- What roles will these individuals play?

- How will growth affect the organizational structure of your business?

- What outside advisors would be of benefit to your business team?

- What role will your board of directors have in your business?

Aerospa

a break from reality

Organizational Plan

Current Plan:

Alex Apelbaum – CEO & President
Store Managers
Store Employees

Future Plan:

Alex Apelbaum – CEO & President
CFO
Expansion/Real Estate VP
Operations VP
Store Managers
Store Employees

Board of Directors:

Faisal Anwar, CEO, Biscuit King
Shirley Lin, Partner, Lin, Lui & Kuhlman
Austin Shau, Chair, Citizens for Mass Transit

The organizational structure of Aerospa will be crucial to its success. Initially, the management team will consist only of Alex Apelbaum. Renovations will be conducted by a subcontractor, as will the initial training of store staff in the fields of massage and salon skills. There will be between five and nine positions available in every store, consisting of one manager and at least four specialists who will be able to conduct both massages and manicures. Specialists will undergo initial training to receive their nail license and be able to administer first rate manicures and massages. Eventually, the management team will include a Chief Financial Officer, an operations officer and an officer with expertise in real estate and expansion issues.

Looking for a new challenge? The Vault Job Board has thousands
of top jobs for all experience levels. Visit www.vault.com.

VAULT CAREER LIBRARY   49

Assessment of risk/competitors

Every new business faces some risk; don't try to make readers of your business plan believe otherwise. If you do not address all of the risks associated with your idea, the reader will assume that you are unaware of any drawbacks and will question your competence. By clearly outlining potential problems in a clear and concise manner and explaining how you plan to overcome them, you will give the reader more confidence than if you had omitted all mention of them. Give a detailed analysis of how you plan to succeed despite the risks associated with the business.

The next step is identifying the companies that will be your competitors. Write about their strengths and weaknesses and how they have created a niche for themselves within the marketplace. People who are interested in becoming part of your business team are going to want to know how you deal with competition.

- What are the risks associated with starting your business?

- What are your competitors doing that is allowing them to make money in the marketplace?

- How are you going to create a niche for your business?

- What competitors pose current or potential threats to your business?

- What will be the response of competitors when you enter the marketplace?

Financial plan

The financial section of your business plan should include your estimated startup costs, projected income statement, balance sheet and projected statement of cash flows. In addition, it should include explanations of any irregularities in your data and the assumptions you used in projecting finances. The financial section of your business plan should demonstrate how your business is going to be profitable. Make sure to explain your reasoning and present the information in a consistent format. Financial professionals can immediately judge your business savvy by the quality of your income statement, balance sheet and statement of cash flows.

Aerospa

a b r e a k   f r o m   r e a l i t y

Assessment of Risk

The risks associated with Aerospa involve airport property development contracts and the probability of competitors once the idea is introduced. Property contracts in airports vary depending on the flow of travelers. Obtaining airport locations may also vary depending on availability and price negotiations. Based on the frequency of flights coming into and out of a particular airport, contracts will tend to be much more expensive in certain areas. Some airports contract out their storefront leases while others fill the stores themselves. Airport property can be charged by square foot, a percentage of sales, or even a combination of the two. These contracts will be vital to the financial success of Aerospa.

If you are not comfortable preparing your own financial statements, seek outside counsel. Tax accountants and financial advisors can help you set up your income statement, balance sheet and statement of cash flows. Make sure you spend the necessary time to make sure that you understand the format.

This section will be the one most carefully scrutinized by investors. If you do not prepare the statements yourself, make sure that whoever did so explains to you and others exactly why each number is there. Potential investors will want to understand every detail in your financial plan. Be prepared to answer every question and provide additional projections and scenarios.

Many venture capitalists are looking for a very high return in the next five to seven years from any business. They will look for certain profit margins and anticipated sales when analyzing your business plan. But don't let that goad you into inflating your figures. Investors have experience in the marketplace and know when predictions are out of line. In fact, if your projections seem unrealistic they have the potential to kill the deal immediately.

Looking for a new challenge? The Vault Job Board has thousands
of top jobs for all experience levels. Visit www.vault.com.

VAULT CAREER LIBRARY   **51**

Aerospa

a   break   from   reality

AEROSPA				
PROJECTED INCOME STATEMENT				
	Month 1	Month 2	Month 3	Month 4	Month 5
Sales 1/3 Capacity	$	$40,850.00	$40,850.00	$40,850.00	$40,850.00
Sales 1/2 Capacity	$	$60,225.00	$60,225.00	$60,225.00	$60,225.00
Sales 3/4 Capacity	$	$90,337.00	$90,337.00	$90,337.00	$90,337.00
***Start-up Costs**	$28,070.00	$	$	$	$
Costs of Goods Sold	$	$456.25	$456.25	$456.25	$456.25
Marketing Materials	$500.00	$500.00	$500.00	$500.00	$500.00
Advertising Expense	$2,000.00	$2,000.00	$2,000.00	$2,000.00	$2,000.00
Benefits	$220.00	$3,300.00	$3,300.00	$3,300.00	$3,300.00
Salaries	$4,333.33	$31,968.00	$31,968.00	$31,968.00	$31,968.00
Telephone	$50.00	$50.00	$50.00	$50.00	$50.00
Virtual Office	$150.00	$150.00	$150.00	$150.00	$150.00
Rent Expense	$2,583.33	$2,583.33	$2,583.33	$2,583.33	$2,583.33
Credit Card Processing	$	$456.25	$456.25	$456.25	$456.25
Monthly Expenses	*$37,903.66*	*$41,463.83*	*$41,463.83*	*$41,463.83*	*$41,463.83*
1/3 Capacity Net Income	$(37,903.66)	$(613.83)	$(613.83)	$(613.83)	$(613.83)
1/3 Capacity YTD	$(37,903.66)	$(38,520.49)	$(39,134.32)	$(39,748.15)	$(40,361.98)
1/2 Capacity Net Income	$(37,903.66)	$18,761.17	$18,761.17	$18,761.17	$18,761.17
1/2 Capacity YTD	$(37,903.66)	$(19,145.49)	$(384.32)	$18.376.85	$37,138.02
3/4 Capacity Net Income	$(37,903.66)	$48,873.17	$48,873.17	$48,873.17	$48,873.17
3/4 Capacity YTD	$(37,903.66)	$10,966.51	$59,839.68	$108,712.85	$157,586.02

Assumptions

*Detailed explanation of start-up costs on following page
Operating capacity based on average $15 services in 15-minute intervals
$31 per square foot – 1000 square foot space
3 Massage Therapists ($10.50/hr + 10% + tips), 3 Manicurists ($7.50/hr + 10% + tips),
1 Manager $7/hr + 2% quarterly bonus.

Financial Plan

AEROSPA						
PROJECTED INCOME STATEMENT						
Month 6	Month 7	Month 8	Month 9	Month 10	Month 11	Month 12
$40,850.00	$40,850.00	$40,850.00	$40,850.00	$40,850.00	$40,850.00	$40,850.00
$60,225.00	$60,225.00	$60,225.00	$60,225.00	$60,225.00	$60,225.00	$60,225.00
$90,337.00	$90,337.00	$90,337.00	$90,337.00	$90,337.00	$90,337.00	$90,337.00
$	$	$	$	$	$	$
$456.25	$456.25	$456.25	$456.25	$456.25	$456.25	$456.25
$500.00	$500.00	$500.00	$500.00	$500.00	$500.00	$500.00
$2,000.00	$2,000.00	$2,000.00	$2,000.00	$2,000.00	$2,000.00	$2,000.00
$3,300.00	$3,300.00	$3,300.00	$3,300.00	$3,300.00	$3,300.00	$3,300.00
$31,968.00	$31,968.00	$31,968.00	$31,968.00	$31,968.00	$31,968.00	$31,968.00
$50.00	$50.00	$50.00	$50.00	$50.00	$50.00	$50.00
$150.00	$150.00	$150.00	$150.00	$150.00	$150.00	$150.00
$2,583.33	$2,583.33	$2,583.33	$2,583.33	$2,583.33	$2,583.33	$2,583.33
$456.25	$456.25	$456.25	$456.25	$456.25	$456.25	$456.25
$41,463.83	$41,463.83	$41,463.83	$41,463.83	$41,463.83	$41,463.83	$41,463.83
$(613.83)	$(613.83)	$(613.83)	$(613.83)	$(613.83)	$(613.83)	$(613.83)
$(40,975.81)	$(41,598.64)	$(42,203.47)	$(42,817.30)	$(43,431.13)	$(44,044.96)	$(44,658.79)
$18,761.17	$18,761.17	$18,761.17	$18,761.17	$18,761.17	$18,761.17	$18,761.17
$55,899.19	$74,660.36	$93,421.53	$112,182.70	$130,943.87	$149,705.04	$168,466.21
$48,873.17	$48,873.17	$48,873.17	$48,873.17	$48,873.17	$48,873.17	$48,873.17
$206,459.19	$206,459.19	$304,205.53	$353,078.70	$401,951.87	$450,825.04	$499,698.21

Looking for a new challenge? The Vault Job Board has thousands
of top jobs for all experience levels. Visit www.vault.com.

VAULT CAREER LIBRARY

53

Aerospa

a break from reality

AEROSPA					
PROJECTED STATEMENT OF CASH FLOWS					
	Month 1	Month 2	Month 3	Month 4	Month 5
Sales 1/3 Capacity	$	$40,850.00	$40,850.00	$40,850.00	$40,850.00
Sales 1/2 Capacity	$	$60,225.00	$60,225.00	$60,225.00	$60,225.00
Sales 3/4 Capacity	$	$90,337.00	$90,337.00	$90,337.00	$90,337.00
Monthly Expenses	$37,903.66	$41,463.83	$41,463.83	$41,463.83	$41,463.83
1/3 Capacity Net Income	$(37,903.66)	$(613.83)	$(613.83)	$(613.83)	$(613.83)
1/3 Capacity YTD	$(37,903.66)	$(38,520.49)	$(39,134.32)	$(39,748.15)	$(40,361.96)
1/2 Capacity Net Income	$(37,903.66)	$18,761.17	$18,761.17	$18,761.17	$18,761.17
1/2 Capacity YTD	$(37,903.66)	$(19,145.49)	$(384.32)	$18,376.85	$37,138.02
3/4 Capacity Net Income	$(37,903.66)	$48,873.17	$48,873.17	$48,873.17	$48,873.17
3/4 Capacity YTD	$(37,903.66)	$10,966.51	$59,839.68	$108,712.85	$157,586.02

Assumptions

3 Massage Therapists ($10.50/hr + 10% + tips), 3 Manicurists ($7.50/hr + 10% + tips),
1 Manager $7/hr + 2% quarterly bonus.

Financial Plan

AEROSPA						
PROJECTED STATEMENT OF CASH FLOWS						
Month 6	**Month 7**	**Month 8**	**Month 9**	**Month 10**	**Month 11**	**Month 12**
$40,850.00	$40,850.00	$40,850.00	$40,850.00	$40,850.00	$40,850.00	$40,850.00
$60,225.00	$60,225.00	$60,225.00	$60,225.00	$60,225.00	$60,225.00	$60,225.00
$90,337.00	$90,337.00	$90,337.00	$90,337.00	$90,337.00	$90,337.00	$90,337.00
$41,463.83	$41,463.83	$41,463.83	$41,463.83	$41,463.83	$41,463.83	$41,463.83
$(613.83)	$(613.83)	$(613.83)	$(613.83)	$(613.83)	$(613.83)	$(613.83)
$(40,975.81)	$(41,598.64)	$(42,203.47)	$(42,817.30)	$(43,431.13)	$(44,044.96)	$(44,658.79)
$18,761.17	$18,761.17	$18,761.17	$18,761.17	$18,761.17	$18,761.17	$18,761.17
$55,899.19	$74,660.36	$93,421.53	$112,182.70	$130,943.87	$149,705.04	$168,466.21
$48,873.17	$48,873.17	$48,873.17	$48,873.17	$48,873.17	$48,873.17	$48,873.17
$206,459.19	$255,332.36	$304,205.53	$353,078.70	$401,951.87	$450,825.04	$499,698.21

Looking for a new challenge? The Vault Job Board has thousands
of top jobs for all experience levels. Visit www.vault.com.

VAULT CAREER LIBRARY   **55**

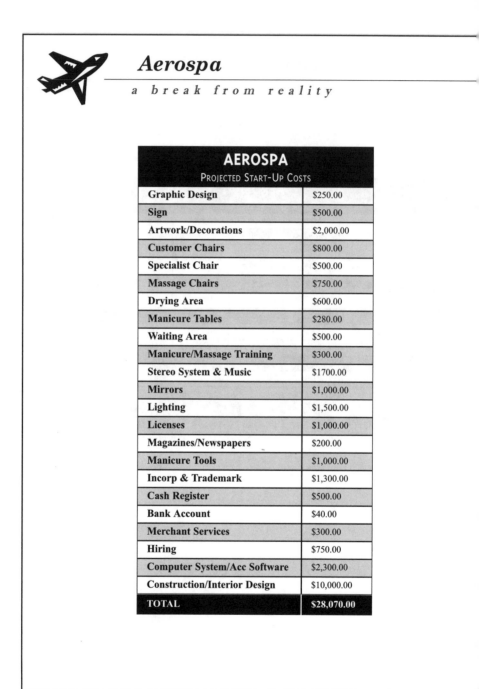

Aerospa

a   break   from   reality

AEROSPA	
PROJECTED START-UP COSTS	
Graphic Design	$250.00
Sign	$500.00
Artwork/Decorations	$2,000.00
Customer Chairs	$800.00
Specialist Chair	$500.00
Massage Chairs	$750.00
Drying Area	$600.00
Manicure Tables	$280.00
Waiting Area	$500.00
Manicure/Massage Training	$300.00
Stereo System & Music	$1700.00
Mirrors	$1,000.00
Lighting	$1,500.00
Licenses	$1,000.00
Magazines/Newspapers	$200.00
Manicure Tools	$1,000.00
Incorp & Trademark	$1,300.00
Cash Register	$500.00
Bank Account	$40.00
Merchant Services	$300.00
Hiring	$750.00
Computer System/Acc Software	$2,300.00
Construction/Interior Design	$10,000.00
TOTAL	$28,070.00

Financial Plan

AEROSPA

PROJECTED BALANCE SHEET
END OF FIRST YEAR

Assets

Current Assets
Cash	$	188,266
Accounts Receivable	$	1,500
Merchandise Inventory	$	500
Supplies	$	200
Total Current Assets	$	190,466

Fixed Assets
Equipment	$	80,000
Less Depreciation	$	0
Total Fixed Assets	$	80,000

Total Assets	**$**	**270,466**

Liabilities and Owner's Equity

Current Liabilities
Accounts Payable	$	2,000
Current Portion of Long-Term Debt	$	0
Total Current Liabilities	$	2,000

Long-Term Liabilities
Notes Payable	$	0
Other Long-Term Liabilities	$	0
Total Long-Term Liabilities	$	0

Owner's Equity
Apelbaum Capital	$	50,000
Investor 1	$	25,000
Investor 2	$	25,000
Retained Earnings	$	168,466
Total Owner's Equity	$	268,466

Total Liabilities and Owner's Equity	**$**	**270,466**

Assumptions:
Numbers based on 1/2 capacity average for year 1

Looking for a new challenge? The Vault Job Board has thousands
of top jobs for all experience levels. Visit www.vault.com.

VAULT CAREER LIBRARY   **57**

Appendix

The appendix portion of your business plan should include any other information that you have discovered while doing research for your business. It can include examples of your competitors, general information on the industry, survey and questionnaire responses, or even testaments from potential customers who think your business is a great idea. While you shouldn't overstuff the appendix, it is a great place to include valuable information that supports your idea and gives the reader further confidence in your business.

It is also a good idea to put in detailed descriptions of some of the main projects planned by your company in the appendix. This will give the reader an opportunity to learn in more detail about your business if he or she desires. The appendix is meant for specific information that is not essential within the body of the business plan.

- What information do you have to include that will help give the reader a better understanding of your business?

- What material do you have that gives the reader some insight into your competitors or potential customers?

Biographies of key personnel

One of the main issues that readers will focus on is the quality of the people involved in your business. When you have a small business, the background of each individual plays a large part in shaping the culture and future of your company. Including information on your company's key personnel will give the reader an idea of the talents and skills that your company possesses. Highlight areas that demonstrate industry expertise and will give your business an advantage in the marketplace. The biographies of key personnel should give the reader an idea of the backgrounds, experience, and specific industry knowledge that each individual adds to the company and the synergy these different experiences will create.

Remember that investors are as interested in the individuals running the company as they are in the actual enterprise. In the end, your people make or break your business.

• What are the backgrounds of the key members of your team?

• What specific experiences have prepared these individuals to be a part of your business?

• How do the skills and talents of your employees give your business an advantage in the marketplace?

Key Points

• Perform in-depth research on the industry you are entering and the competitors currently in the marketplace.

• Have your business plan tell a story.

• Present your business plan in a creative way that grabs the attention of the reader.

• Present your financial statements in a professional way that is accepted under Generally Accepted Accounting Principles.

• Make realistic projections about the future success of your business.

• Focus on the comparative advantage of your company throughout the entire business plan.

• Highlight all resources and contacts that will help you make your business a success.

Looking for a new challenge? The Vault Job Board has thousands
of top jobs for all experience levels. Visit www.vault.com.

VAULT CAREER LIBRARY   59

Use the Internet's
MOST TARGETED
job search tools.

Vault Job Board

Target your search by industry, function, and experience level, and find the job openings that you want.

VaultMatch Resume Database

Vault takes match-making to the next level: post your resume and customize your search by industry, function, experience and more. We'll match job listings with your interests and criteria and e-mail them directly to your inbox.

VAULT
> the insider career network™

Marketing &
Advertising Strategy

No matter how advantageous a product or service you have, if no one knows about it, your business will not succeed. An effective marketing campaign should focus on several basic ideas: the competitive advantages your business provides to the consumer, the type of customer to target, and the best method of conveying your advantages to this group of people. Marketing your product to consumers is about creating the right type of image for your business in the marketplace. Advertising is about finding the right medium to connect with your potential customers and convincing them of the comparative advantage of your product or service.

Your marketing strategy should be to create an identifiable image that customers can relate to. A large part of your marketing efforts will be focused on the name of your business, your logo, and any slogan you have created. Whether you decide to do it yourself or use an advertising agency, there are certain key concepts to keep in mind. Your advertisements should deliver a clear and identifiable message that readers can relate to. Well-designed advertisements catch the eye and stay in the brain. Make your advertisements unique in every possible way.

But remember that the simplest form of advertising is also the most powerful. No matter how large your business becomes, word-of-mouth advertising will remain your most effective marketing tool. Understanding that basic tenet, you should make sure every customer is extremely satisfied. Go the extra mile in providing top-notch service. Give your customers comment cards so they can remark on what they like and what could be done differently. Create satisfied customers and they will come back time and time again – and bring their friends.

The first part of this chapter will discuss the process of formulating a marketing strategy; the second will examine the various advertising media available.

- How do your competitors market and advertise their products and services?

- What will the name, slogan, and logo of your business be?

Looking for a new challenge? The Vault Job Board has thousands
of top jobs for all experience levels. Visit www.vault.com.

VAULT CAREER LIBRARY   61

- What message do these three key elements of the marketing and advertising campaigns convey?

- Why are people are going to want to purchase your product or service?

- What is the most effective way for you to reach your target audience?

- What preferences, desires, and similarities does your target audience share?

- How will you conduct your advertising campaign?

- What image will you be trying to create through your marketing?

- What people can help you market and advertise your product or service?

Market research

The first step in developing a marketing strategy is to conduct thorough market research. Having a comprehensive understanding of current market initiatives and possible future advancements will allow you to position your company appropriately. As a start, test your competitors' products and services. Fill out your own internal customer evaluation forms for each of the products or services of the companies you test. Also, don't forget to test your own business; the best way to critique any business is to become a customer. Have your employees do the same.

Take the time to sit with a customer if he or she has a complaint or an idea on how to improve your business. Then adopt the best techniques and ideas you find. Eliminate the disappointing aspects of other businesses and develop your own image, emphasizing the comparative advantage of your business.

Not only should you analyze your competitors' products and operations, but you should also observe their marketing initiatives. Track the way they advertise their product or service. What type of image do they project?

You should also learn about the community in which you are going to be conducting business. Become involved in community affairs, take part in philanthropic events and donate to local charities. This will both help you understand your market (you could learn, for example, on which kiosks you would do best to post flyers), and create a positive image for your company. The best way to create barriers of entry to future competitors is to position your business as the local favorite.

- What resources will help you conduct market research?

- What industry contacts and other key people will help you to get an understanding for the marketplace?

- What companies do you need to learn about to get an understanding for the marketplace?

- What historical trends have shaped the current landscape of the marketplace?

- What future developments will have an impact in changing the way business is conducted?

- How can you allocate the necessary resources to research and development to consistently remain one step ahead of the competition?

- What other influences in the marketplace will have an impact on your business?

- How will you incorporate the personal preferences and patterns of consumers into your market research analysis?

Reaching the target market

Your business will achieve its best results if you focus efforts on a specific target market, instead of spewing out a barrage of unfocused techniques. The initial months and years of starting a company are critical in the formation of a solid foundation for your business – there is no time to experiment with frivolous expenditures that don't produce. Still, you should take advantage of low-cost methods that allow you to test the waters in different markets.

The best way to reach your target market is to conduct a survey of a wide variety of people and determine what type of person is most likely to purchase your product or service. In addition, focus on what it will take to expand interest in your product or service to other people. Although your marketing and advertising efforts should be focused on a target market, you want to create as large a market as possible by offering different variations of your product and service for different types of people. Surveys of your friends, workers, potential customers, competitor customers and random people will help you create the largest and most well-defined target market for your business.

Looking for a new challenge? The Vault Job Board has thousands
of top jobs for all experience levels. Visit www.vault.com.

VAULT CAREER LIBRARY   63

- What is the target market of your business?

- Are there ways to create variations to your product or service to expand the target market?

- Through what advertising media will you reach your target market?

- What evaluations and surveys will you conduct to understand how to make your product or service the best available to your target market?

- Who can you get to try the products and services of your competitors and evaluate them?

- What is the general image that each of your competitors project?

- How will you market the difference between your company and the competitors?

- What type of people will most readily identify with this difference?

Competitive advantage

Just as your business idea is based on your competitive advantage in the marketplace, so should your advertising and marketing strategy. By focusing on this competitive advantage in your marketing, you will create a clear message to potential customers about your business.

Focus on an easy-to-understand image that represents the strengths of your product or service. Then create an advertising campaign that both focuses on your competitive advantage and appeals to your target market.

- What is the competitive advantage of your business?

- In what ways will the competitive advantage of your business make the consumer crave your product or service?

- What target market will benefit the most from the competitive advantage of your business?

- How will you maintain this competitive advantage?

- How will you seek to develop other competitive advantages?

- How can you convey your competitive advantage in a marketing campaign?

- How can you convey your competitive advantage in an advertising campaign?

Press releases

Press releases and subsequent exposure in the media are an excellent way to attract attention to your business. Stories, or even short blurbs, about your business in local and national publications or TV news programs will give you excellent exposure, helping to lend credibility to your company.

There are a couple of ways to get press releases to the media. The first is simply to do it yourself. Create a clear, concise, and engrossing publicity piece. Include a letter to the editor describing why the publication and its readers will be interested in your article. The other way is to hire a service to distribute press releases for you. There are services available on the Web that will do this for under $200. If you have enough cash, of course, you can hire an outside public relations agency to handle the whole process: writing the releases, sending them out, and then hounding the editors with follow-up phone calls.

If your business is Internet-based, media coverage is an excellent way to draw web surfers to your location. Advertising strictly online, through such options as search engines and banners, will generally not draw a large enough audience to your site.

For many types of businesses, the most active, educated and vocal consumers in the marketplace – and the most important people to reach – are so-called "industry experts" who either work in the media, or are commonly cited by pundits. Establishing a credible and solid reputation with these core people will help get your business off to the right start.

Issue press releases for every conceivable situation: when you open your business, when you form a partnership with another company, when you sponsor something in the community or when you introduce a new variation to a product or service. Using press releases to get the word out about your business is an ongoing process that will involve buddying up with contacts in the media. (This is why hiring public relations specialists who already have such contacts is often a good idea.) Journalists are constantly looking for new ways to obtain information, so these relationships with the press will be mutually beneficial. Get out your backscratcher!

- What publications will your target market be reading?

- Who do you know at various news publications?

Looking for a new challenge? The Vault Job Board has thousands
of top jobs for all experience levels. Visit www.vault.com.

VAULT CAREER LIBRARY   65

- What contacts do you have that could put you in touch with key people at various publications?

- How can your business benefit from press releases?

- What news do you have to announce in a press release?

Advertising options

There are a plethora of advertising venues open to your nascent business. The key is selecting the right medium for your target audience. Trying to reach teenagers by advertising on *60 Minutes*, for example, is futile.

Certain grassroots advertising methods are commonly used, regardless of the advertising and marketing budget of the business. Offer features that will attract the type of individual that would most likely benefit from your product or service. Something as simple as offering free coffee or donuts every morning will help to attract a loyal customer base. Showing you care about the customers is the way to attract a consistent customer base and benefit from their referrals.

Every product, brochure, business card, pizza box or other document that you provide to potential or existing customers should have the name of your business, phone number, web site, e-mail address and general information about your company. In addition, every piece of literature should request feedback from your customers (though this might be tough on a business card). Even though advertisements are meant to attract business, consumers will react more favorably when you solicit their opinions.

When deciding which advertising media to use, it is important to approximate the returns from the campaign. When buying advertising space or time, request numbers on approximately how many individuals the vehicle will reach (based on subscriptions, number of listeners to a radio show, "hits" on a web site, etc.). But you should not assume that just because your message reaches many people through a certain vehicle, that it is an effective form of advertising. The goal is to select the advertising meda with the greatest rate of return; in order to make sure you are doing this, you have to keep track of what forms of advertising get the best response. You do this by asking your customers.

As new technologies and vehicles for advertising evolve, it is important to continuously update your advertising efforts to expand your target market –

and to keep your audience, who may be changing their advertising-consumption habits (moving from print media to the Web, for example). Just as you should study the trends in your industry, you should study advertising and marketing trends.

Finally, you should continue advertising no matter how large a client base or how successful you become. Hugely successful companies like Intel and Procter & Gamble still spend hundreds of millions of dollars each year on advertising. They know that, with the explosion of brand options, consumers are more fickle today than ever.

- How much do you have to spend on your advertising budget?

- What media will be the most effective way of reaching your target market?

- What media will be the most cost-effective way of reaching your target market?

- If price were no option, how would you advertise your product or service?

- How can other individuals and companies help in your advertising efforts?

- What will be the message of your advertisements?

- What publications does your target market subscribe to?

- How does your target market spend their free time?

- When is the most opportune time to reach your target market?

- What is the demographic of the people you are trying to reach?

- Who are the industry specialists in the marketplace?

- What people do you know that can help spread the word about the new product or service you are offering?

Print

Newspapers, magazines, newsletters and other printed publications are some of the most common advertising media. However, advertisements in the most widely read publications can be extremely costly. Figure out which publications will reach your target audience most efficiently. Trade journals and other reports specific to your industry are an excellent way to ensure that

Looking for a new challenge? The Vault Job Board has thousands of top jobs for all experience levels. Visit www.vault.com.

VAULT CAREER LIBRARY

67

you reach a target market, since they are designed to reach a very narrow group of people. If such a publication exists for your industry, it represents an excellent advertising opportunity.

- What types of print publications will be beneficial for your company to advertise in?

- Which of these are the most cost-effective for your business?

- What rate of return do you expect from advertising in the different publications?

- Which publication best focuses on your target market?

Newspapers

Newspapers generally attract a diverse audience, and thus may not be the best advertising option if your business targets a narrow market. On the upside, because most newspapers have a solid reputation for accuracy, advertising in a newspaper is a good way to establish credibility for your business and reach a diverse group of people. Newspapers such as *The New York Times*, *The Washington Post*, *The Wall Street Journal*, and *The Los Angeles Times* can afford to charge a lot for their advertising space because they are widely read and are guaranteed to reach a very large audience. If you are just starting out, you will probably not be able to afford these astronomical rates. Fortunately, smaller newspapers often actually do a better job of reaching a certain demographic of individuals. Target newspapers that distribute in areas where your desired market resides; you can find this out by contacting a newspaper and asking for a breakdown of its circulation.

- What are the best newspapers that reach your target market?

- What are the most cost-effective newspapers that reach your target market?

- What are the costs of advertising at different newspapers?

- Does it make more sense for you to run a larger ad in one newspaper instead of a smaller one at another?

- What demographic and number of readers does each newspaper reach?

- How can you make your advertisement attract the attention of readers and entice them to seek more information?

Magazines

Although the magazine industry has been shrinking for some time, it is still an excellent advertising venue. Many print magazines are now available online; others are solely available on the Web. Like the major newspapers, major magazines such as *BusinessWeek*, *Time*, *Life*, *Newsweek*, *Forbes* and others will probably be out of your price range, at first. But there are other, cheaper options. It is important to find a magazine that has established a credible reputation and developed a solid reader base. If a magazine only has an online presence, it is essential to find out how many hits it gets per month and from what demographics.

Make sure your magazine advertisement stands out. You may want to consider getting a larger and more colorful ad in a smaller magazine than a drab little corner in a major one. Most readers don't scour every square inch of their magazines.

- What magazines best reach your target market?

- What are the prices of different advertising options in each of these magazines?

- How can you make your advertisement stand out and catch the attention of the reader?

- How many magazines are distributed and where?

Direct mail

Although a direct mailing can be quite costly, it is a reliable way to reach your target market. Even if you just send out a postcard that has your web address and a phone number for more information, a direct mailing can be an excellent way to jumpstart your business. To start, keep and compile the names and addresses of your customers and put them on your mailing list. Repeat customers will be your best source of business. By notifying them of new products and services through direct mailings, you keep them coming back for more.

To do a direct mailing, you must have accurate names, titles, addresses, and phone numbers. One of the major problems with direct mailings is that they only hit their target individual roughly half of the time – people move, mailing lists are inaccurate, etc. – and even if they reach their recipients, most direct mailings swiftly find their way to the trash. How to avoid this dread

Looking for a new challenge? The Vault Job Board has thousands of top jobs for all experience levels. Visit www.vault.com.

VAULT CAREER LIBRARY   69

fate? First, identify the exact person that you are trying to reach and his or her title. Second, make sure your mailing is attractive and looks important. Direct mailings have often been dubbed "junk mail" because of their drab omnipresence. Your direct mailing should be professional in appearance and describe your business in a succinct manner. Go the extra step. Create a professional piece that makes the reader want to find out more about your business.

There are ways to make your direct mailings more effective. There are many places to get mailing lists and business addresses, but many are outdated or inaccurate. Ensure the accuracy of the addresses you have been supplied before committing to a mailing. Follow-up phone calls are an excellent way to ensure that the person received the piece; you can then answer any questions he or she may have.

• How will you get the names and addresses for a direct mailing?

• How do you plan to make your direct mailing look professional and important?

• What information will you provide in your direct mailing?

• How will you follow up on your direct mailing to enhance your response rate?

Radio

Attract your customers over the airwaves! Commuters often listen to the radio during their morning trip to work. Others put the radio on while relaxing at home, driving or lounging at the beach. Some workplaces have the radio blaring all day. Advertising on the radio can be a highly effective way to entice listeners to find out more information on your business.

Radio stations usually sell time blocks of between thirty seconds and a minute and a half. Your advertisement should be informative, non-annoying, succinct, and accurately describe your product or service. Flashes of humor will make listeners pay closer attention. Provide an easily remembered phone number or Web address and repeat it often.

• What AM or FM radio stations does your target market listen to?

• What are the advantages of radio advertising?

• How much revenue do you anticipate generating from radio advertising?

Television

Americans watch more television than ever before, using it as a primary source for news and entertainment. It's also a source for product and service information; TV time is crammed with advertisements for just about everything that can be legally sold, rented or hired. Many businesses have televisions available for their customers while they shop, too - there's no escaping the TV. Tapping into this venue can be a great way to get the word out about your company.

The visual component helps make TV ads more effective than radio, so be sure that any commercial you produce takes advantage of this. Viewers should be left with an image of your product or service, or of your company in general, and that image should be positive. Buying TV ads is more complicated than radio advertising, however, and is also typically much more expensive. Advertisers need to choose between advertising nationally for the broadest reach (and greatest cost) or with a local network affiliate to save money and focus on a particular region. You generally choose to advertise during a particular program, targeting the shows that are most popular with your target audience. It can also be expensive to film and create an effective television ad.

Ad spots on TV are typically 15 or 30 seconds in length; a rare few run as long as a minute. The shorter the ad, the cheaper it is to purchase airtime. Another option is the so-called "infomercial," where you purchase an entire programming block (half an hour or more) and produce a business-focused program to run in that time slot. Most infomercials run during off-peak viewing hours, making them more affordable than you might otherwise think.

• In what ways would a TV commercial be more effective than a radio ad?

• How can you catch the audience's attention in 30 seconds or less?

• What stations or network affiliates would you approach to buy airtime?

• What programs are most popular with your target market?

• How will you create the television ad?

Looking for a new challenge? The Vault Job Board has thousands
of top jobs for all experience levels. Visit www.vault.com.

VAULT CAREER LIBRARY   71

Into the great wide open

Go outdoors to advertise. Everything from posting flyers in town to renting billboard space on major highways can provide excellent opportunities to reach your market. For example, many businesses that cater to professionals in major cities advertise on the trains, subways, and platforms where they wait glumly for transportation.

- Where are individuals in your target market most apt to see outdoor advertising?

- What forms of outdoor advertising would be cost-effective for your business?

Event sponsorship

Whether you contribute money, time or non-cash resources, event sponsorship is a great way to reach a group of people gathered for the same reason. Understanding that those attending an event have come together for the same reason is the key to event sponsorship: you must decide whether this group of people falls within your target market. If chosen correctly, the events you sponsor will not only give you increased exposure to your target market, but may also provide you with valuable contacts.

- What types of events does your target market frequent?

- What can you donate to sponsor an event?

- What sponsors have these events had in the past?

- What contacts and resources will sponsoring this event put your business in touch with?

Low-cost advertising

Advertising doesn't have to cost a lot of money to work. Most business owners start out strapped for cash and must rely on their creativity to get the word out. These cash-poor innovators often hit on new methods of advertising that are later adopted by other businesses. Making cold calls, handing out brochures, and posting flyers may all be good ways to spread the word about your business.

• What resources can you take advantage of to advertise your business for little to no cost?

Partnerships

Another excellent way to advertise your business is through partnerships. By teaming up with another company, you gain access to their entire target market and reach a new segment of the population. Finding companies with complementary interests to your business is essential to making a good partnership.

Another plus is that under these arrangements, you usually do not pay anything. Instead, you offer something of value to the other business.

• How can your business use partnerships to increase exposure and enhance sales?

• What businesses have complementary interests and would make good partners?

• What can your business offer another company in the way of a partnership?

Get online

The Web is another available advertising platform. In fact, there are so many ways to advertise online, it's easy for your ad to get lost in the cyberjungle. Discovering how to target your market online is essential.

Take time to research how online advertising can increase your business. Getting a sense of where the future of online advertising is heading will help focus your efforts in the right direction. Currently, comparable advertisements in print and other media are much more expensive because of their proven track record, but online advertising is expected to become more expensive in the coming years. Incorporating online advertising into your advertising plan from the start will help you gauge the amount you should spend on it in the future.

Both businesses and advertising agencies are currently in a dilemma over how best to benefit from online advertising. The success of your online advertisement is determined by the "click-through" rate. This indicates how many people actually clicked on your advertisement to find out more about

Looking for a new challenge? The Vault Job Board has thousands
of top jobs for all experience levels. Visit www.vault.com.

VAULT CAREER LIBRARY   73

your business. You should also find out how many people actually visited the web page where your advertisement is located (a measure called impressions).

Although banner ads are currently one of the most popular online advertising methods, their click through rates are often very low. A new form of advertising percolating in the online world is interstitial marketing. These two strategies will be discussed later in this chapter, but know that over the next couple of years new and perhaps more effective methods of Internet advertising will no doubt emerge.

- How can your business use online advertising to reach potential customers?

- How can you interest people to click your advertisement to find out more information on your business?

- What methods of online advertising have you seen that enticed you to find out more information?

- Does your target market use the Internet?

- Is your target market comfortable making purchases using the Internet?

Create a corporate web site

Creating a web site for your company is increasingly crucial for conducting business today. As the world becomes more comfortable with e-commerce, more and more business will be conducted on the Internet. Although it is not essential to be able to sell on your web site immediately – you could set up a site simply for exposure – you should plan to open your site to e-commerce as soon as possible. Why? A web site with e-commerce is a store that's open and accessible seven days a week, 24 hours a day.

To create a web site, you have to find a host server. This means you have to find a service that will actually post your web page. It usually costs only twenty or thirty dollars a month for basic hosting services; there are a plethora of other options available to you for additional cost, but the basic service is usually sufficient for startups. There are even services that will host your web site for free, though not normally as a direct link. Thus, free hosting is at best a temporary solution. When setting up your site, choose and register a domain name that is easy for your customers to remember and applicable to your business.

Although professional web design help is available and should be used in some circumstances, there are a lot of programs available to help you easily create a web site by yourself. Don't be intimidated by the apparent complexity of web site creation. Several retail software packages make the process simple. Talk to other business owners to see how they set up their web sites.

Some business use their web site as their main store. By allowing customers to conduct business online, there is no need to have a physical store, unless you are providing products or services that must be seen in person. Company web sites allow you to create a "virtual store" that can interact with potential customers, provide more information, and even conduct sales.

Make sure that your web site is user friendly and easy to navigate. Having too many graphics or complicated interfaces will make your site slow and frustrating. Because web surfers are fickle, you must keep them interested with quick page loads, attractive visuals and useful information. It is good to also have links to other pages that contain information pertinent to the customer. Links represent an excellent way to provide content for your customers and can be used to create valuable partnerships.

- What sort of information will you provide on your web site?

- Will you be able to conduct sales using your web site?

- What links will you have on your web site?

- How will you build your site?

- What hosting options will you explore?

- What might you choose for a domain name?

Search engines

Many people use search engines to find different sites for information they are looking for. These engines sort through all of the web sites available and then report which ones are most applicable to a surfer's query. Examples of search engines include Google, Yahoo and Alta Vista. The ever-increasing amount of information on the Web makes search engines a frequent first stop for web surfers. Registering your web site on these engines is therefore essential.

Looking for a new challenge? The Vault Job Board has thousands of top jobs for all experience levels. Visit www.vault.com.

VAULT CAREER LIBRARY   75

There are a couple of ways to get your site listed on these search engines. Services such as Microsoft's Submit It! register your web site with the search engines for a nominal price. Otherwise, you can register with an engine yourself by going to the search engine's main page, and clicking on "add URL," or "add this site to Lycos," etc. Your web address and description of your site should contain key words that will correlate with searches performed by your target market. You can also pay to add your company to search sites like Google.

- Which search engines are popular with your target market?

- How will you register your web site with the search engines?

Banners

Banners, which provide a link to the web site of the advertiser, were one of the first and most popular forms of advertising on the Web. These ads are often animated, blink beseechingly, and can even make sounds in an attempt to entice viewers to find out more information.

For the time being, banners will continue to be a major source of advertising revenue. Once your web site is up and running, selling banner space is an excellent way for you to generate extra revenue. You may also wish to partner with other businesses and trade banners on each other's sites; choose web sites frequently visited by your target audience. As with all forms of advertising, doing your homework on the medium's audience will ensure you get the most out of your banner advertising.

- What web sites does your target market view on a regular basis?

- How will I make my banner enticing enough to get viewers to click on it?

- What partnerships can I form to trade banners with other businesses?

Popups and interstitials

Popups and interstitial advertising are two alternatives to banner ads. Popups open a new browser window containing the advertisement, including a link to the company's page. Interstitials are pages that are displayed for a brief period in the main browser window while the user waits for a new page to load; think of them as the Internet equivalent to a stopover on a long flight.

Both force the viewer to focus on a full-page advertisement before returning to the regular contents of the web site.

Interstitials and popups are effective because of their intrusiveness - the viewer has no choice but to read the advertisement before continuing on to another web page. This gives each form of advertising an advantage over the more passive method of banner ads. Many people object to this level of intrusiveness, however, and users can download free programs to prevent popups from popping up. Despite this, they remain a popular and effective means of advertising on the Web.

- How can you use interstitial and popup advertising to benefit your business?

- How will the development of new advertising methods help you promote your business on the Web?

- How can you keep abreast of developments in Internet advertising to decide when the time is right for your business to take part?

- What sort of content can you add to your popups and interstitials to make them more of an attraction than a nuisance for viewers?

Links

Links, which move viewers from one web page to another with a simple click of the mouse, are an excellent way to attract viewers to your web site. The more places you can stamp your name on the web, the better your chances are for attracting viewers. Links are also a great way to begin forming relationships with other businesses in the online community.

- What businesses can you promote to trade links to each other's web site?

- What type of web site is not a competitor of yours but also appeals to your target market?

E-commerce

Consumers are increasingly drawn to the ease of shopping online. E-commerce allows customers to make purchases around the clock, and without dealing with another human. Businesses also save on personnel and store space costs. One of the most important issues of e-commerce is creating a secure transaction of personal information over the Internet. Although

Looking for a new challenge? The Vault Job Board has thousands
of top jobs for all experience levels. Visit www.vault.com.

VAULT CAREER LIBRARY 77

Internet security has improved vastly in recent years, (some research indicates that it is safer than handing your credit card to a store clerk) it will be some time before the general public is comfortable sending their credit card numbers into cyberspace. Nonetheless, many web sites are giving customers the option of shopping online. Even large car manufacturers are creating online test drives and ways to customize car purchases over the Internet. Although it may take a while before people are willing to buy cars over the Internet, big business is adjusting the effect e-commerce has had on the marketplace, and on its bottom line.

- How comfortable is your target market with the World Wide Web?

- How can you make your web site friendly to e-commerce?

- How can you make customers comfortable making a purchase online?

- How will your business benefit from e-commerce?

Add it up

The distribution of their advertising dollars is a constant obsession for entrepreneurs. The goal is to spend an amount at which returns exceed the initial advertising expenditure. As you experiment, you will find that certain methods work better than others for you. With this information in hand you should change your mix of advertising methods. Finding the right ways to advertise is essential to building your image and reputation. Remember that the most expensive advertising methods are not always the ones that produce the best results. Take the time to research the different advertising methods available to your business and to track how your initiatives are working.

- How much money do you have to spend on advertising?

- Which advertising medium will create the most exposure for your business?

- How can you develop a good mix of different advertising techniques that fits within your budget?

- In what ways can you increase business exposure that will not cost any money?

Key points

- Use a variety of advertising methods to promote your business.

- Remember that word of mouth is the most effective form of advertising.

- Create an identifiable logo and company name.

- Create the type of image that your target market will want to be associated with.

- Be creative and innovative in your presentation.

- Use partnerships and joint ventures to promote your business.

- Remember that your business is best promoted using both traditional and online advertising.

- Experiment with different types of advertising media to find out which work best for your business.

Looking for a new challenge? The Vault Job Board has thousands
of top jobs for all experience levels. Visit www.vault.com.

VAULT CAREER LIBRARY   **79**

Managing Your Business

CHAPTER 6

You're the boss

Leading a company is not easy work. You are responsible for absolutely everything that happens. However, taking on this responsibility and succeeding is one of the most gratifying parts of being an entrepreneur. In order to manage your business properly, it is a good idea for you to learn and understand each of the necessary operations of the business. If you are starting a business alone, you will automatically have to fill the role of president, treasurer, advertising director, operations manager and many others. If you are starting a business with other people (whether partners or employees), it is worth the time to become acquainted with the roles of each individual at your company. Having an overall understanding for every facet of your business will allow you to better communicate your thoughts and insights to other team members. However, you should keep in mind that your main responsibility in running a company is to make money. As the leader of your company, you must be the one to steer it in the right direction and determine when it may be time to change course. You are the final decision-maker and the ultimate authority on all issues.

- What personal skills do you possess that will help you to be an effective manager?

- What roles will you be required to fill in your new business?

- How will you manage your employees to gain their trust, respect, and loyalty?

- What is your vision for the future of your company?

The basics of management

Managing your business requires creating a team of individuals that works together efficiently to add value to the business. Have a vision for your team and create goals that will take you in the right direction. Reward employees for their work and encourage them to offer suggestions and criticism. As your business grows, there will be new responsibilities and facets that require additional attention and resources – and additional employees. Developing

Looking for a new challenge? The Vault Job Board has thousands of top jobs for all experience levels. Visit www.vault.com.

VAULT CAREER LIBRARY   81

an effective methodology for managing all of this is essential to the success of your company.

- What vision do you have for the future of your business?

- How will you instill in your employees the same desire you have for your business to succeed?

- What do you see as the major components of managing your business?

- What principles do you believe will help to effectively manage your employees and your business as it grows?

Master of your domain

When setting up your business, it is important to delegate responsibility to other members of the company. In doing so, you will be able to relieve yourself of some tasks to focus on other areas of importance. Make a list of the different categories that need to be addressed (i.e. financial, marketing, operations, legal). Then pick appropriate people to head up these posts. Hiring the right type of employees and delegating responsibility are crucial parts of starting your business. Make sure to spend plenty of time getting to know these people as workers and individuals before making them part of the team. When possible, try to look for people who have experience in your area of business. This will help jumpstart your operation and increase your speed on the road to success.

- Who will be responsible for the various areas of your business?

- What can you delegate to others to free up time to spend focusing on the core areas of your business?

- How will you effectively manage your time to make sure that you can devote attention to the different aspects of your business?

Assessing needs

Although personnel needs of your business will be in constant flux, proper planning will ensure that you are able to take advantage of the abilities of your employees in the most efficient manner. Utilizing the personnel you currently have available to you will cut down on your hiring needs. Rotating employees through different roles will familiarize your workers with the different parts of your company and make them comfortable with multiple responsibilities. This will also help each employee understand the roles of their peers and be able to offer valuable advice on many different subjects. Contributing employees are happy employees. Happy employees mean lower turnover for you.

Every member of your business team has different strengths. Identifying those strengths and the areas where you need to bring in help is crucial. By taking a step back and reviewing where your company is heading on at least a quarterly basis, you will be able to better gauge the needs and opportunities for your business.

- What are the current personnel needs of your business?

- What are the strengths of your business team?

- What are some weaknesses that you need to fix in order to maximize your performance?

- How will you educate employees to learn multiple responsibilities so they can perform more efficiently as a group?

Board of directors

The board of directors of a company must meet on at least an annual basis to view the operations of the business, make suggestions and come up with ideas. Although the board meets infrequently, you should be able to contact them on a regular basis to get feedback and advice. For your board of directors, you should choose individuals with industry experience, who can provide guidance, prestige and ideas for your business.

- What individuals do you know personally who you can approach to become board members of your business?

- What individuals that you do not know would have valuable advice and contacts that will help your business?

- What will be the role of the board of directors?

Experience

Experience is an important element of every business. Having experience in a given industry provides you with the necessary skills to interpret market data and forecast future trends. If you are fairly new to the industry, there are

Looking for a new challenge? The Vault Job Board has thousands
of top jobs for all experience levels. Visit www.vault.com.

VAULT CAREER LIBRARY   83

many ways to gain expertise. You can hire an experienced individual, hire an outside consultant or learn everything by yourself. In addition, consult with your board members and outside advisors that have industry experience.

There are two schools of thought about experience when hiring individuals. First, if a person does have experience in a given industry, he or she will be able to hit the ground running and draw on industry knowledge and contacts. The downside for hiring an experienced person is that they cost more. On the other hand, inexperienced individuals can be molded to your needs and specifications, cost less and may be more loyal. But, what you save in money may be lost in training time. Measure these two options carefully. Whether you hire experienced or green employees, you must continue to train them, through attending seminars, continuing education classes or even holding your own workshops. Experienced, savvy workers are an important part of developing a superior company that can conduct business in an efficient and profitable manner and develop into an industry leader.

- What experience do you bring to your business?

- What experience do your board members and outside advisors have?

- What experience level are you looking for in employees?

- How do you plan on using the experience of your team to leverage your business?

Hiring personnel

Your new employees should complement you and the other employees. If you get frustrated with details and are not a "numbers person," hire someone who understands financial statements and has some background in the financial industry. If you are a numbers guru and lack the creative talent necessary to market your product or service, look to hire someone that has experience in advertising or marketing to help promote your business.

All of your employees should be able to handle multiple tasks and have the desire to learn. And they should all have some sales skills. Every person in a startup – from the assistants to the president – needs to be able to sell the product or service to those that they meet. Each of your employees should be a walking promotion for your business.

Spending the appropriate amount of time to find the right individuals to become part of your team is essential to the success of your business. There are many ways to find the best employees: word of mouth, hiring agencies, ads in your local newspaper, job web sites or even flyers you can post yourself.

One of the most frustrating problems every small business owner experiences is lack of staff to handle the ever-increasing workload. Explosive company growth is fantastic, but you must be able to handle this growth without overtaxing your current staff. Don't rush out and hire anyone that can fill the role, but rather find the best individuals to fill your openings in a timely manner. It is imperative not to compromise your requirements and standards by bringing someone in too soon. Finding the right balance between growth, hiring the right people and keeping your current staff is one key to maintaining your business.

Finding qualified employees

Where do you find qualified workers? While many companies still rely on help wanted ads in the local newspaper, the best employees are increasingly finding jobs online. One of the most effective ways to located qualified employees is to use an electronic recruiting service, which screens a database of job seekers to find those candidates whose interests and qualifications match your available position.

- How will you find qualified employees?

- How many employees do you need for your business?

- What roles do you expect them to fill?

- What qualifications and experience are you looking for?

Creating vested interest in the company

It is essential to give your employees a vested interest in the success of your business. In many companies today, employees feel unimportant, and that they have nothing to gain from the success of the firm. That's why bonuses, ESOP plans, and other incentives should be part of every business. When individuals have tangible reasons to work harder, they are more likely to share your enthusiasm and desire for the company to succeed. It is amazing how much effort, initiative and intensity people are willing to provide when they have a stake in the outcome.

Looking for a new challenge? The Vault Job Board has thousands of top jobs for all experience levels. Visit www.vault.com.

VAULT CAREER LIBRARY   **85**

Employees should have other incentives besides money to work hard and give back to the business; your employees should enjoy what they're doing. Create a friendly and caring atmosphere at work with special benefits for your employees. Sometimes a little perk can create an incredible atmosphere of warmth and friendliness. Whether you try casual days, birthday cakes, family days, pet days, surprise bonuses, pizza parties or special days off, do something different at work to make your employees feel like they are part of a company that cares about them. An atmosphere of caring isn't confined just to little perks: sponsor local community events, send employees back for continuing education, recognize the families of your employees. These extra touches will create a positive working atmosphere that will have you and the rest of your team looking forward to coming to work every day.

- How can you give your employees a vested interest in your business?

- What other ways can you provide for your employees?

- What can you do to give your staff the highest level of personal satisfaction for a job well done?

Important employee responsibilities

An important part of managing your business is relinquishing responsibility to others. Giving employees significant responsibility not only makes them feel important, but also frees up time so you can focus on growing your business. It can be very difficult to let go of certain tasks that you have performed from day one; however, being a manager means delegating responsibility in the most efficient manner, allowing you to spend time on the core areas of the business. Releasing the operational and financial aspects of the business will allow you to focus on future initiatives and other opportunities in the marketplace.

Utilize your employees to the best of their abilities. Push employees to expand their horizons and learn about different aspects of the company. Encourage them to form goals that will advance their professional abilities and make a significant impact on the company. Reward your employees for doing well, providing an idea for a project or working longer hours to finish particular projects. Recognizing the efforts of your employees is an important part of creating a strong bond of respect and communication.

Always keep the lines of communication open and encourage employees to come up with new ideas and suggestions, even on topics not directly related to what they are doing. Keep your employees in the loop. In many growing companies, employees often feel in the dark about the way the business is growing. This can result in an uneasy and speculative workforce and even drive individuals to leave the company. Keep your employees feeling like they are an integral part of the team by actively communicating with them, encouraging them to take their skills to the next level, giving them important responsibilities within the business and letting them know they are important to the company and to you personally.

- How will you delegate responsibilities in a way that will allow you to focus on the core areas of your business?

- What areas of your business are critical and need your constant attention?

- How do you plan to make your employees feel like valuable members of the team?

Incentives & benefits

There are many different types of incentives and benefits packages that you can make available to your employees. Unless you only have part-time employees, your staff will want a medical benefits plan. Offering a comprehensive medical benefits package is extremely helpful when hiring skilled workers. Offering a tuition reimbursement program will encourage employees to increase their knowledge with continuing education classes and advanced degrees. Encouraging your employees to take financial or computer literacy classes will also add value to your company. Stock options can be especially helpful when trying to hire an individual whose current salary you may not be able to match. The future value of the stock options may be enough to interest them into coming aboard. Bonus plans are another excellent way to reward employees for their good work. Make sure to explain to employees the basis for their bonus. It is a good idea to tie bonuses to personal as well as company performance.

- How will offering benefits and incentives improve your business team?

- What programs do you plan to provide for your employees?

- How do you plan to reward employees for the financial success of the business?

Looking for a new challenge? The Vault Job Board has thousands
of top jobs for all experience levels. Visit www.vault.com.

VAULT CAREER LIBRARY   **87**

Team concept

Building a business team that works well together is an essential part of the success of any group. Finding the personalities and skill sets that fit is an important part of the hiring process. Creating an invigorating atmosphere, encouraging people to work together, and providing strong leadership and guidance are all essential parts of building a winning team.

- In what ways can you build a cohesive team within your company?

- How can you encourage employees to learn about each other's different roles?

- What personalities and skill sets will you look for in potential members of your business team?

Employee rotation programs

Having employees experience different parts of the business is a great way to create a better level of understanding and efficiency among them. By rotating employees into different jobs, you increase the learning curves of each individual and get a different perspective on how to maximize the performance of each position. This will also give your employees a higher sense of self-worth as they will understand the overall process of your business. Having multifaceted employees can be especially helpful when a member of your team is sick or leaves the company. Because other people have been trained for the job as well, it will be easier to cover for this person.

- What are the different functions within your business?

- What is a good amount of time for each individual to spend rotating through a certain job while not letting productivity suffer?

- How can you encourage employees to contribute new ideas and suggestions they have from their new experiences?

Internal & external classes

Encouraging your employees to take classes is a great way for them to improve their skills and provide better work for your business. Take advantage of the educational institutions in your area. Work to create a reimbursement program for your employees for some or all of the costs associated with the classes. Put together a recommended list of classes and then discuss them with your employees. Another great way to train your employees is to offer internal classes at work. Have individuals with extensive knowledge in certain areas offer short half-hour classes dealing with their areas of expertise.

Types of classes

There are three main areas for employees to enhance their skills: product skills, professional skills and computer skills.

Product skills classes should educate individuals on a certain industry, product or service applicable to your business. These classes are best for individuals who need to learn more about your industry or need a better sense of the role your business plays in the marketplace. For example, advertising professionals would benefit from marketing classes, while financial professionals would benefit from taking business and accounting classes.

Professional skills, such as presentation skills and management techniques are imperative to the success of your business. The demeanor and actions of each employee should project and enhance your company's image. Most people not native to the business world need help fine-tuning their professional skills. Have exemplary employees offer short classes on some of these topics or find programs offered at local schools.

The desktop computer has revolutionized the way business is conducted. Still, most people do not know how to use computers to their full capacity. Encourage your employees to improve their computer skills with additional classes and even tutorials available online. Enhanced computer skills will increase the efficiency and productivity of each individual employee at your business.

- What product skills classes would benefit individuals at your company?

- What professional skills should you fine tune?

- What computer programs should you learn more about?

- Which individuals within your business would benefit most from these classes?

- Which employees can teach internal classes on product knowledge, computer skills, or professional skills?

Looking for a new challenge? The Vault Job Board has thousands
of top jobs for all experience levels. Visit www.vault.com.

VAULT CAREER LIBRARY   89

- What are the goals you hope to attain from offering continuing education to your employees?

- How much are you willing to invest in both time and dollars to make sure your company is as technologically advanced as your competitors?

Set aside time to brainstorm

As discussed earlier, brainstorming on a regular basis is an important way to come up with new product and service ideas, ways for your business to perform more efficiently and other new ideas that will enhance revenue and profit. While it can be difficult to find time to set aside for brainstorming when you are a small business owner, the long-term benefits of doing so will have a positive impact on the future success of your company.

- What areas of your business would benefit from brainstorming?

- What other individuals would be valuable additions to the brainstorming team?

- What current parts of your business do you think you can improve?

New ideas for your business

The most successful companies in the world, like GM, Ford, Microsoft, IBM and Nike, are constantly looking for new ways to conduct business and new products to sell. Auto manufacturers force themselves to come up with new ideas for their cars on an annual basis. Software manufacturers have to continue to come up with new products or variations on existing ones if they expect to stay in business. Clothing manufacturers have to keep pace with or create new styles and trends.

No matter what industry you are in, it is imperative to continue to come up with new ideas for your business. Having someone spend time on research and development is essential to understanding what types of ideas will work and how to implement them. Encourage your employees to generate new ideas. Reward them for trying even if their ideas are not used. The benefits from the few that do work will far outweigh the cost and time it took to come up with the ones that do not.

• What ideas do you currently have for your business that you are not implementing?

• How will the future of the industry affect the way you conduct business?

• How can you encourage your employees to come up with new ideas for the business?

Efficiency evaluation

Running your business in an efficient manner will save you time, resources and, ultimately, money. Owning up-to-date computers, software, telephones and other equipment will allow your business to operate at an efficient level. Businesses that are equipped with the proper resources and know how to use them can do the same amount of work as inefficient companies twice their size. Using up-to-date computers and other telecommunications equipment is just one way that your business can operate efficiently. Also determine how much time each of your employees is spending doing certain tasks. If there is one project that takes an extraordinary amount of time, it may make more sense to hire another employee, outsource it or even hire a temporary worker.

• Are your employees spending too much time on certain projects?

• Are your computers and software enabling your employees to work at their optimal level of output?

• What resources are available to your business that will allow you to function in a more efficient manner?

• Will outsourcing work or bringing in temporary help work best for certain projects?

Managing growth

As your business grows, you will be responsible for making sure that you remain profitable as your sales increase. One of the most common reasons businesses fail is that management has not been able to handle the needs brought on by growth. Avoid this through proper planning and evaluation. This will help you realize when you are growing out of your current resources and when it is time to add on to your company. Installing the proper procedures from the beginning will ensure that you stay on top of your growth.

Looking for a new challenge? The Vault Job Board has thousands
of top jobs for all experience levels. Visit www.vault.com.

VAULT CAREER LIBRARY   **91**

Getting feedback from your employees is another way to understand current workload demands and areas with potential for rapid growth. Employees are often on the front line of dealing with current issues within your company. They know firsthand whether they have too much work or how customers are reacting. Keeping an eye on the growth rate of your company will also help you pinpoint underperforming areas of your business.

- How will you know when your business has outgrown its current resources?

- How often do you consult your employees regarding these matters?

- How can you start planning now for your company's growth?

- What programs will you create to obtain a constant flow of feedback from your employees?

Negotiation

Management involves negotiation with clients, employees and customers; being a manager entails a never-ending set of negotiations. There are a number of books that detail how to negotiate and "beat" your opponent. But the fact is, the only way a negotiation can be successful is if both sides walk away with a feeling of accomplishment. You never want the other side to feel they got a bad bargain because they will never want to do business with you again. Successful negotiations form a bond of trust that will create future possibilities for doing business together. The only good deal is a fair deal.

Before the start of any negotiation, decide what you want and what you think the other side is interested in. Outline what you want to discuss and solve. If you are negotiating with another company, make sure you are meeting with someone who has the authority to make decisions, or you might be wasting your time. Try and find a way to give the other side what it desires while also fulfilling your own needs.

- What is it you want to gain from the negotiation?

- What is it the other side is looking to gain?

- Do you understand the reasoning of the other side?

- How can you make your negotiations successful for both sides if at all possible?

Growth capital

As your business grows, you will need additional capital to expand your operations. The key is to avoid having a cash crunch – a situation when your company is growing but does not have the extra cash to handle the additional business. Cash crunches are a common failure of small businesses. To counteract this possibility, always have a ready line of credit. Whether you have personal funds available, ties to a venture capitalist or investors that are willing to kick in more money, being prepared will ensure that your business can continue to grow in an efficient manner.

- Who will you rely on for cash when your business needs extra money?

- How will increases in revenue affect the need for additional resources and cash outlay?

- How will entering new lines of business and making the necessary purchases to compete in this market affect your cash flow?

Key Points

- Always be on the lookout for new opportunities.

- Find ways to make your employees truly feel part of the team, and create an environment where they are excited to come to work every day.

- Hire individuals who bring new skills and exciting perspectives to your business to broaden your knowledge.

- Always encourage employees to express new ideas and suggestions for doing things differently.

- Continuously look for ways to better your business and become more efficient.

- Always produce work that you are proud of and that satisfies customers beyond their needs. If you are not happy with it, rest assured your customers will feel the same way.

- Encourage your employees to continue their education and improve their skill sets.

- Give your employees a vested interest in the success of your business.

- Put in place procedures that will allow you to monitor how the growth of your business affects your resources.

Looking for a new challenge? The Vault Job Board has thousands of top jobs for all experience levels. Visit www.vault.com.

VAULT CAREER LIBRARY   **93**

Use the Internet's
MOST TARGETED
job search tools.

Vault Job Board

Target your search by industry, function, and experience level, and find the job openings that you want.

VaultMatch Resume Database

Vault takes match-making to the next level: post your resume and customize your search by industry, function, experience and more. We'll match job listings with your interests and criteria and e-mail them directly to your inbox.

VΛULT
> the insider career network™

Financial, Legal & Tax Issues

CHAPTER 7

Money, that's what I want

Financial planning is critical to the health and success of your company. Obtaining the proper amount of start-up capital is crucial to building a solid foundation for your business. Many businesses underestimate the amount of money they will need and are unable to adequately grow as a result. Properly estimating the amount of money you will need to start and grow your business is a difficult task, because there are always unanticipated costs.

Your financial plan should consist of projected startup costs, estimated cash flow and a projected income statement; this section will help take you through the fundamentals. First, get an idea for the approximate costs associated with your type of business by analyzing your competitors. Then, raise enough capital to get you through the first few slow months. Preparing your estimated financial statements in the right manner will help you to understand how much money you will need and will impress potential investors.

Getting financing is the challenge of all entrepreneurs. To raise money, you must be able to convince another group of individuals of the merits and potential of your idea. Seeking investors can be a discouraging process. Howard Schultz, founder of coffeehouse giant Starbucks, met with over 100 individuals before he was able to convince enough people to invest in his idea to start his business. He remained upbeat and confident in his idea. Ultimately, the investors invested more in Schultz than his actual idea. Investors are looking for good ideas that have potential, but the savvy investor knows that the idea is just one part of the equation. They look for passionate people who believe in their idea and will do whatever it takes to make the idea succeed. Convey your passion and vision for your business.

- Are you going to need to raise money to start your business?

- If so, what type of financing are you looking to obtain (debt, equity)?

- What do you see as the biggest financial challenges to starting your business?

- How will you effectively deal with these issues?

- Who do you know to help you prepare your financial plan?

Estimating start-up costs

Estimating the total costs of starting your business is tough. You can assume certain overhead expenses such as incorporation, business cards and letterhead, and some form of communication, such as a phone or e-mail account. After that, you can customize the needs of your business as necessary. Many Internet businesses avoid incurring the costs of a retail space by conducting business solely on their web site and buying direct from the manufacturers. Other businesses find that hiring freelancers reduces employee costs.

A partial list of startup costs:

- Graphic design
- Legal services
- Office furniture
- Office supplies
- Letterhead
- Business cards
- Hiring costs

- Employee salaries and benefits
- Travel
- Advertising
- Inventory
- Computer hardware
- Software

Although not all of these are applicable to every business, it is a good idea to consider and write down all of the costs associated with the type of business you are starting. When starting your business it is essential to maximize every resource available to you and cut costs wherever possible. Effective use of your funds will allow you to spend more money in areas such as advertising, research and development.

- What items will you need to start your business?

- How much money will you need to start your business?

- What will be your approximate overhead and monthly expenses?

- What other companies can you analyze to get a better idea of your costs?

- What are the approximate expenses incurred by other companies in your industry?

- What entrepreneurs can advise you and help you comprehend some of the general start-up costs?

Break-even analysis

Understanding what it will take to put your business "in the black" is very important to potential investors, partners and anyone who has a financial stake in the company – particularly you. There may be a fair amount of lag time before your firm turns a profit. Even stock market darling America Online has only recently turned a profit. Yet the company has been in the limelight for some time, due to the extensive partnerships, explosive growth and solid image the firm has created. These relationships and positioning have proven to be instrumental to the company's success.

It is important to build a solid foundation, create distribution channels, and promote the image of your business when you are first starting. Even if your company is extremely profitable from the beginning, it is wise to invest your money back into the business. Becoming profitable should be one of the main goals of your business, but it is equally important to build the proper infrastructure that will grow with your company and allow it to prosper.

Make sure that anyone who invests money in your business understands your expectations and plans. If you expect to run "in the red" for an extensive period of time, make sure you can explain to your investors why this is the case. Often, although a company may not be profitable, the value it has created (in brand recognition, for example) will produce additional revenue in the future. By making sure that individuals with a stake in the financial future of your company understand your financial reasoning, you will be able to build a solid foundation positioned for success.

- How long do you anticipate it will take for your company to turn a profit?

- How long can your business afford to run at a deficit before additional financing is needed?

- What can you do to add future value to your company?

- How long can you personally afford to live with your company "in the red"?

- How do you plan to reinvest profits back into your company?

- Have you informed all of your investors as to whether profits will be distributed or reinvested?

Looking for a new challenge? The Vault Job Board has thousands
of top jobs for all experience levels. Visit www.vault.com.

VAULT CAREER LIBRARY   **97**

Potential investors

Choosing the right type of people to help finance your business is an extremely important step. Although a person may be willing to invest in your business or loan you money, there may be strings attached that make the offer undesirable. Make sure that you are comfortable with all of the people that become financially involved in your business. Establish precisely what their involvement and expectations will be before they invest any money. Draft legal documents that validate the agreement. Whether these individuals are friends, family, bank officers, venture capitalists or angels, it is important to communicate the financial plan and vision for the future of your business.

Look for individuals who understand the nature of your business, have realistic expectations and will allow you to run your own business. Someone that wants to become too involved in the everyday decision making process may overshadow your own thoughts and visions for your company – the very reason you want to be an entrepreneur! Finding people that understand the ups and downs of starting a business and will work with you to make the company a success is also vital. Time spent worrying about investors backing out is time and mental energy wasted.

- How would you describe your ideal investor?

- What characteristics would make an individual not fit your profile?

- What level of decision-making power do you want your investors to have?

- What will entice an individual to invest in your company?

- What are you giving this individual for their investment?

Debt versus equity financing

The main types of financing are debt and equity. Equity is ownership in the business; debt is money that must be paid back with interest in the future. Examples of debt instruments are bank loans, personal loans and bonds. Stocks and any other form of investment that receives an ownership position is considered equity. When individuals receive equity in your company they are receiving partial ownership. If you incur debt to finance your business you are not losing any ownership, but you must pay back the principal of the loan, plus interest.

Debt financing is attractive because in taking on loans, you do not lose any ownership in your company. If you are able to get a loan for $100,000 at a 7 percent interest rate over five years, and anticipate your company will generate enough profit to make the payments, debt instruments are very appealing. But if you should be unable to pay even one of your monthly loan payments, you will be forced to either obtain the money from someone else (because a bank will not make you another loan), declare bankruptcy or sell the business. It can be very difficult to get a loan for your business. If your credit report is bad or if you do not have enough assets or collateral to securitize the loan, you may need to seek equity financing.

Equity investors often want a management/advisory position in the company. Whether such arrangements are palatable will vary depending on the size of the investment and your need for capital. Most entrepreneurs want to keep as much control over their business as possible.

A good mix of debt and equity financing makes sense for most businesses. Even if you are able to completely finance the business from your personal savings, it's smart to start establishing credit with a bank. Once your business grows and your capital expenditures increase, you will be able to secure a larger line of credit. It takes time to build your line of credit with a bank, no matter how well your business is doing.

- What is your ideal combination of debt and equity in your business?

- How large a loan will you be able to take out?

- How much ownership do you wish to retain in the business?

Cash flow

The cash flow of your business plays a large role in being able to operate at your maximum level of efficiency. Many companies have cash flow problems even when they are making money and growing. Cash flow problems can arise from rapid growth, a delay in accounts receivable (payment for purchases), slow business or unforeseen expenses. Having ready cash on hand helps alleviate these woes. However, having too much cash sitting in your business bank account is not a wise use of funds. Avoid this problem by having a steady line of capital available to your business if you need it. Whether this capital comes from investors who have expressed an eagerness to invest more money or from a line of credit you have

Looking for a new challenge? The Vault Job Board has thousands of top jobs for all experience levels. Visit www.vault.com.

VAULT CAREER LIBRARY   99

established with the bank, having access to funds will allow your business to continue operating without delay.

Many companies experience cash flow problems due to rapid growth. There could be worse problems! Yet if you do not have access to funds to fuel this growth, your business will not be able to take advantage of the opportunities that present themselves.

- What access do you have to additional financing?

- How long do your customers have to pay for products/services rendered?

- What events will adversely affect your cash flow?

Financial statements

The key financial statements of your business are the income statement, balance sheet and statement of cash flows. These three items will all be carefully scrutinized. Preparing these statements in a generally accepted accounting format will ensure that your financial plan is presented in a professional manner. Preparing them can be tough for someone without formal financial and accounting training. If you are not comfortable with preparing them yourself, an accountant or corporate finance professional can help guide you. However, it is recommended that you also learn how to create these statements for yourself.

Be aware that there are many different ways to present each one of these statements. As your business grows, you should hire an experienced accountant to help you present your numbers in the most effective way. Most local universities offer classes that explain the fundamentals of income statements, balance sheets, and cash flow statements. It is important that you understand the general underpinnings of each of these statements because they are the raw indicators of the success of your business.

- How much experience have you had with preparing financial statements?

- Who can help you prepare these documents?

- How will you educate yourself to have a better understanding of financial statements?

Income statement

The income statement is a summary of sales and expenses for a given period. This statement reports the profitability of your business. In preparing the income statement, sales must be calculated monthly for a year. Since you are just starting your business, it is a good idea to forecast sales by using expert opinions, sales reports from comparable businesses or surveys of consumer spending patterns. It can be expected that your sales will be lower in your first few months of operation. Adjust the numbers to show a realistic increase in sales as the year progresses. Sales will likely be the major source of revenue on the income statement. The rest of the numbers will be expenses like salary and wages, cost of goods sold (COGS), selling expenses, advertising, office expenses, taxes, insurance, rent and other miscellaneous expenses.

In addition to listing month-by-month projections for your first year of business, list projections for the second and third years as well. Investors generally want to understand how you plan to grow the business and what will fuel increased revenue and profits. It is essential to make realistic, research-backed projections. Also, describe two or three different scenarios for your business based on different assumptions. Since these are estimates, it is a good idea to give the reader an idea of multiple possibilities.

The activities of your business will change the net results of your income statement on a daily basis. It is preferable to prepare your income statement on a monthly schedule, but you should at the very least prepare the statements quarterly. This will give you an understanding of how your business is doing and what expenses may need to be altered. In addition, as your business grows there may be additional capital expenditures, loans taken out or hiring expenses that alter the bottom line in the short term, but pay huge dividends in the end. When this is the case, use depreciation and other accounting techniques to calculate a more realistic earnings estimate.

Preparing an income statement can be instructive. By understanding the way different costs interrelate and affect the bottom line, you will be able to make adjustments and increase your profit.

- What research will give you an understanding of the general spending patterns of consumers in your industry?

- What other companies in your industry can you use to fine-tune your estimates?

Looking for a new challenge? The Vault Job Board has thousands
of top jobs for all experience levels. Visit www.vault.com.

VAULT CAREER LIBRARY   **101**

Statement of cash flows

The statement of cash flows reports the difference between actual cash receipts and cash payments. Another way to look at this is that the statement of cash flows reflects changes in the balance sheet. The statement of cash flows is different than the income statement; where the income statement reflects profit, the statement of cash flows displays the amount of cash available to your business at a given moment. Adjustments to the cash flow statement are made only when physical cash is received or paid out. This makes it very difficult to create a cash flow statement before your business is actually generating revenue. (This is where the term "creative accounting" comes from.) Nevertheless, it is crucial that you gain an understanding of the cash flow situation of your business.

It is also important to make monthly projections for the statement of cash flows. The first few months on the statement of cash flows reflect the outlay of costs associated with starting the business. Several figures from the income statement are placed directly on the statement of cash flows, with adjustments made when necessary for cash payments and receivables not yet made. If your cash flow balance is negative, then your business must borrow money to cover the disbursements. If your balance is extremely high, you may look to invest some of your money in short term investment vehicles. Once again, it is a good idea to list several different cash flow scenarios. Estimates are very difficult to make and it is better to give the reader multiple possible outcomes.

Cash flow plays a very important role in all businesses, but can have an even more dramatic effect on startups. Even profitable businesses that are growing rapidly can fail due to lack of available funds. Use the sample statement of cash flows in the appendix to get an idea of how to prepare your business.

- Will you receive payment in any form that will delay the amount of time before you receive the physical cash?

- What resources will you have available when you need to raise additional cash?

Balance sheet

The balance sheet is a snapshot of your business at a given moment in time. It summarizes the assets, liabilities, shareholders' equity and net worth of the business. The balance sheet is generally constructed at the end of the year.

To produce an estimated balance sheet for the end of the first year, you will have to rely on numbers from the statement of cash flows and income statement.

On the balance sheet, assets equal liabilities plus shareholders' equity. Assets are everything that is owned by the business including inventory, supplies, "guest worker," cash, and property, plant and equipment (PPE). Assets are classified as either current (anything expected to be converted to cash within a year) or fixed (those items which are tangible and will be used for an extended period of time). Liabilities represent everything owed to creditors and include accounts payable, notes payable and portions of long-term debt. Liabilities are classified as either short-term or long-term, depending on when payment is expected. Shareholder's equity represents the net worth of the business. It is the difference between the assets and the liabilities. Examples of shareholders' equity are initial investments made in the business and any profit made from the business (classified as retained earnings).

The balance sheet is an accurate picture of the net worth of your business. It differs from the statement of cash flows and income statement because the balance sheet does not cover a period of time, rather it depicts a given moment.

- What do you envision will be the state of your business one year after the start date?

- What investments have been made in the business?

- What physical assets will have been purchased?

- What liabilities will you have?

Personal savings

The first place to look for financing is your own personal savings. If you are able to finance your own venture, you will be able to retain 100 percent ownership of your business. Unfortunately, most of the time it is very difficult to finance your venture entirely by yourself. Regardless of how you obtain financing, it is always important to invest some amount of your own money in your business. Investors are always cautious of individuals who do not commit any of their own funds. By putting as much money as you are comfortable with into your business, you are showing the investors that you have confidence that the investment will yield a high return.

Looking for a new challenge? The Vault Job Board has thousands
of top jobs for all experience levels. Visit www.vault.com.

VAULT CAREER LIBRARY   **103**

Investing personal savings is always a touchy issue; you do not want to invest so much money that you put a strain on your own personal financial situation. Although there are financial sacrifices that need to be made when starting a business, if you do not have immediate cash available, do not liquidate your assets, take a second mortgage on your home or put yourself under any other unnecessary financial strains. Instead, look for ways to raise money using these items as collateral, or raise the money in some manner that will keep you from being financially overextended.

Map out your personal financial situation for the next six months to a year and determine the appropriate amount you can afford to invest. Invest an amount that will let you keep an adequate percentage of ownership, and that does not put you into excessive debt.

- How much money can you afford to invest without straining your personal finances?

- How much revenue must your business produce to maintain your current standard of living?

Family and friends

Family and friends are another excellent source of capital when starting a business. However, it is never worthwhile to jeopardize a personal relationship. Make sure to put everything in writing, no matter how trivial it may seem. This will help to alleviate any misunderstanding that may come about in the future. It is important to treat any investor in your business, no matter what their relationship to you, in the same professional manner.

- What friends and family members can you approach to help you in your business?

- How will you keep them from feeling obligated or pressured?

Credit cards

A somewhat risky, yet often successful, method for financing your business is credit cards. By taking advantage of the monthly billing cycles, balance transfers and other special promotions offered by credit card companies, many entrepreneurs have successfully started their businesses with plastic. The obvious downside is the accumulation of debt, high interest rates and potentially bad credit if you are unable to make the minimum payment. If you do decide to "max out" your credit cards to raise money to start your business, make sure you understand the payment cycles, interest rates and balance transfer programs offered by the major credit cards. Although there are more traditional sources of financing, credit cards are a viable option and have produced successful results for many entrepreneurs.

- Which major credit cards have the best finance charges?

- Are there any credit cards that cater to small business owners and will actually extend a line of credit with special features?

- How long will it take you to pay off these debts?

- How will you stay on top of what you owe on each card and ensure that you do not become too heavily indebted?

Bank loans

Bank loans are one of the more traditional debt financing methods for small businesses. When you take out a bank loan, each payment period you are required to pay back principal plus interest on the loan. Unfortunately, unless you have an established credit history, items to serve as collateral and strong personal finances, getting a bank loan can be rather difficult. (It is often much easier to get a Small Business Administration (SBA) loan, which is covered in the next section.) However, traditional bank loans often offer the best rates and payment periods. The other benefit of taking out a bank loan is the credit history you are establishing. Once you have successfully displayed your ability to pay off that loan, you will have a much easier time taking out additional loans or applying for a line of credit. This will be extremely helpful as your business grows and you need additional financing to cover additional expenditures. To apply for a bank loan, simply go to your local bank, fill out the necessary papers and wait for the results.

- Do you have a strong credit history?

- Do you have items to serve as collateral for the loan?

- Have you ever applied for a loan before?

Looking for a new challenge? The Vault Job Board has thousands
of top jobs for all experience levels. Visit www.vault.com.

VAULT CAREER LIBRARY   105

The Small Business Administration

The federal Small Business Administration (SBA) was established in 1953 to aid, counsel and protect the interests of the nation's small business community. The SBA offers a variety of resources to entrepreneurs and small business owners. Working with intermediaries, banks and other lending institutions, the SBA encourages and promotes loans and venture capital financing to small businesses. The SBA offers several small business loans through the 7(a) Loan Guaranty and Certified Development Company programs. In addition, the organization helps its clients secure venture capital financing through the Small Business Investment Company Program. The Small Business Administration also funds small loans (up to $25,000) to new businesses. The program is an excellent resource for all entrepreneurs and small business owners that can provide help during many stages of your business. They're on your side!

The Small Business Administration offers the following programs to help entrepreneurs and small business owners finance their business.

- SBA's 7(a) Loan Guaranty Program (General Business)

- SBA's Microloan Program

- SBA's 504 Certified Development Company Program

- SBA's Certified and Preferred Lenders Program

- SBA's Secondary Market Program

- SBA's Surety Bond Program

- Opportunities – Procurement Assistance and Grants

- Financing Your Business workshops

- Shareware programs

In addition, the SBA provides a Directory of Small Business Lending Reported by Commercial Banks and ready-to-complete loan application forms for downloading to your computer (access them at www.sba.gov).

Most lenders are familiar with SBA loan programs. Interested applicants should contact their local lender for further information and assistance in the SBA loan application process. Information on SBA loan programs, management counseling and training services offered by the agency is also available from your local SBA office.

Determining which type of SBA loan is best for your business can be confusing. The following section is a synopsis of the different loan programs backed by the Small Business Administration.

The programs include:

7(a) Loan Guaranty
The 7(a) Loan Guaranty Program is one of the SBA's primary lending programs. It provides loans to small businesses unable to secure financing on reasonable terms through normal lending channels. The program operates through private-sector lenders that provide loans which are, in turn, guaranteed by the SBA (which has no funds for direct lending or grants).

Specialized 7(a): LowDoc
Designed to increase the availability of funds under $150,000 and streamline/expedite the loan review process.

SBA *Express*
Designed to increase the capital available to businesses seeking loans up to $250,000.

CAPLines
An umbrella program to help small businesses meet their short-term and cyclical working capital needs with five separate programs.

Specialized 7(a): International Trade
If your business is preparing to engage or is already engaged in international trade, or is adversely affected by competition from imports, the International Trade Loan Program is designed for you.

Export Working Capital
Designed to provide short-term working capital to exporters in a combined effort of the SBA and the Export-Import Bank.

Pollution Control
Designed to provide loan guarantees to eligible small business for the financing of the planning, design, or installation of a pollution control facility.

Looking for a new challenge? The Vault Job Board has thousands of top jobs for all experience levels. Visit www.vault.com.

VAULT CAREER LIBRARY   **107**

Specialized 7(a): DELTA

Defense Loan and Technical Assistance is a joint SBA and Department of Defense effort to provide financial and technical assistance to small firms adversely affected by cutbacks in defense.

Specialized 7(a): Minority and Women's Prequal

A pilot program that uses intermediaries to assist prospective minority and women borrowers in developing viable loan application packages and securing loans.

Veteran's Loans and Disabled Assistance

The SBA has not been providided funds for direct aid to veterans or the disabled. However both groups are eligible for all SBA loan guaranty programs, and may recieve special consideration.

Qualified Employee Trusts

Provides financial assistance to Employee Stock Ownership Programs (ESOP).

Microloan Program

This program works through intermediaries to provide small loans of as little as $100 up to $35,000.

Certified Development Company (504 Loan) Program

This program, commonly referred to as the 504 program, makes long term loans available for purchasing land, buildings, machinery and equipment, and for building, modernizing or renovating existing facilities and sites.

The Angel Capital Electronic Network

The SBA also offers a program called The Angel Capital Electronic Network (ACE-Net). ACE-Net is a nationwide Internet-based listing service that provides information to angel investors (individual investors who are generally hands-off and have investments in many different startups) on small, dynamic, growing businesses seeking $250,000 to $5 million in equity financing. ACE-Net, sponsored by the Office of Advocacy of the U.S. Small Business Administration, was announced by President Clinton in October 1996. It is a major effort by the Office of Advocacy to systematize, and expand, on a nationwide basis, information available to investors on firms seeking equity financing. ACE-Net is run as a private, independent, not-for-profit organization.

The SBA offers many other excellent financing, startup and consulting resources to entrepreneurs and small business owners. The best way to take advantage of these resources is to schedule a meeting at a branch in your area.

- What resources does the SBA offer that can benefit your business?

- Where is the closest SBA branch office?

Direct public offering (DPO)

Direct public offerings are gaining popularity as financing vehicles for entrepreneurs and small business owners. The Small Corporate Offering Registration (SCOR) was developed by the Securities & Exchange Commission (SEC) in 1992 as a way to help small businesses gain easier access to equity capital while satisfying SEC requirements. The goal of SCOR is to create a filing process simple enough for an entrepreneur, corporate attorney and accountant, yet thorough enough for full disclosure.

SCOR offers small businesses a low-cost, minimal-hassle alternative to filing a traditional initial public offering (IPO) or private placement (PPO). SCOR caters to entrepreneurs, promoters, attorneys and accountants who are not specialists in the securities industry. Under this program, businesses can raise up to $1 million in equity capital annually by selling stock, options, warrants, rights, notes or other debt securities. SCORs provide many advantages over traditional IPOs and PPOs for entrepreneurs: they allow companies to gain access to greater amounts of capital, alter the share price, control costs, select shareholders, create a direct relationship with the shareholders and customize their financing needs.

To become a part of the SCOR program, companies are required to file two forms, the SCOR Form U-7 and Form D. Form U-7 was developed specifically for SCOR and serves as the primary registration document. The Form U-7 must be filed with each state in which you plan to sell securities, and you must file the Form D with the SEC.

Filing a SCOR is far less expensive than a traditional IPO. Initial public offerings can cost $350,000, if not more, in registration, legal and consultant costs. Because they eliminate the need for expensive advisors and cut down on the number of hours spent preparing documents, SCORs can often be filed

Looking for a new challenge? The Vault Job Board has thousands
of top jobs for all experience levels. Visit www.vault.com.

VAULT CAREER LIBRARY   **109**

for under $10,000. Filing a SCOR is also significantly less restrictive than filing for a traditional IPO. Stock sold under a SCOR can be traded in the secondary market. This makes the investment more liquid and less risky, and helps to attract investors.

While the SCOR process is considered simple compared to the other public offering options, there is relatively little instructional information available. Denver-based DataMerge Inc. produces a manual/software program titled "Self-directed IPO, Raising Capital with SCOR," divided into the SCOR Registration Guide and the SCOR Marketing Guide, that walks companies through the filing process with instructions, tips and sample U-7 forms. This provides background on the SCOR process and its evolution, step-by-step instructions for filling out Form U-7, sales/marketing techniques, samples of successfully completed registrations and timetables of events. For more information about the SCOR program and DataMerge's SCOR manual, call (800) 580-1188 or visit www.datamerge.com/scor.html.

- Would your business benefit from a direct public offering?

- How would you market your DPO to potential investors?

Angels

Angels are independently wealthy individuals who invest in different business opportunities. Every entrepreneur dreams of finding an angel that will invest in his or her company, provide advice, and open up a world of connections. Every angel has a different investment philosophy. Some will want to participate in the activities of the business, while others will prefer to stay in the shadows. But don't confuse these angels with their celestial namesakes – they want something in return. Angels are astute businesspeople who have "been around the block" once or twice. They understand how to tie their compensation to the overall success of the business. These savvy investors don't hope to make money on a loan with quarterly payments. Rather, they expect your business to make it big, and for them to be rewarded when it does. Programs such as the SBA-sponsored ACE-Net and other angel networking programs offer fine ways to position yourself to be touched by an angel.

- What individuals do you know who could put you in touch with an angel?

- How can you locate potential angels?

Venture capital

A bitter wag once dubbed venture capital "vulture capital," because venture capitalists sometimes take most of the firm they finance. However, this is not always the case, and venture capitalists, who routinely invest in entrepreneurial business concerns, can provide excellent financing opportunities. In addition, these business groups often provide support and will help you to make industry contacts. Resources such as these can prove to be invaluable. Finding venture capitalists who will be interested in your business and make a valuable contribution takes time, stamina and a little bit of luck.

Obtaining venture capital can be very difficult. To be a candidate, your business must meet specific criteria; most venture capital firms have a model that allows them to sort through the numerous business plans they receive on a daily basis. Based on your business idea, your qualifications and personality, your industry, expected revenue and the amount of financing desired, venture capitalists judge whether to take a deeper look at your company. If they smell a possible fit, the firm will usually invite you to present your business at greater length. After several meetings, adjustments in the financial statements and many hypothetical conversations, the venture capitalists will decide whether to present you with an offer. Do not be afraid to ask for adjustments or turn down the offer. If the requirements of the deal make you uncomfortable, it is not worth forming a partnership.

There are a couple of well-known publications that are excellent places to begin your search for venture capital firms. *Pratt's Guide to Venture Capital*, *Galante's Venture Capital Guide* and numerous other online and print publications separate the different firms into investment type, amount available and industries of interest. It is standard practice to send your business plan and a cover letter to venture capital firms that may be interested in your company. Start with a mailing to the top ten firms that you feel represent the best fit. Once you have exhausted these possibilities, move down the list to other venture capital firms. You may be surprised at who is interested in helping you finance your business.

Present your idea to venture capitalists in a way that shows your qualifications, desire, research and your idea's potential value. The firms that agree with you will be most likely to provide you with the necessary resources and support to help make your business a success.

Looking for a new challenge? The Vault Job Board has thousands of top jobs for all experience levels. Visit www.vault.com.

VAULT CAREER LIBRARY   111

- Do you or any of your business associates have contacts at venture capital firms?

- What sort of investment and equity position are you looking for from a venture capital firm?

- What makes your business idea different from the hundreds that pass across the desk of a venture capitalist on a weekly basis?

Legal and tax issues

All entrepreneurs face legal and tax issues when starting their businesses that lead them to hire professional help. Addressing these issues is one of the less glamorous and interesting parts of starting a business, but proper attention to these issues can save you an incredible amount of time, money and headaches in the long run. Having professional legal advice helps ensure that that your company conducts business in a way that minimizes exposure to legal action. And by having an accountant help you prepare estimated forecasts and financial statements, you will be able to understand the numbers and how they are affecting the performance of your business. Legal and tax issues are very important to establishing a solid foundation from which to build your company.

- In what ways can legal advice help me?

- How will an accountant be able to help me better plan for the growth of my business?

Legal counsel

Choosing the right legal counsel to represent your business is an important step in building your business team. Finding an individual that understands your industry, connects with you on a personal level and has the time to devote to your company will help to minimize some of the risk associated with starting a business. Depending on the type of business you are starting, copyright and patent possibilities, licensing arrangements, organizational structure and other situations that require legal advice, there will be times when you need the services of a lawyer more than others. As it can cost a lot of money to retain strong representation, you may want to offer your potential lawyer shares in your business. This will reduce the amount of actual cash you will have to pay and give the individual a vested interest in the success of your company. If you employ a large law firm, take care that your business does not end up in the hands of a junior lawyer with little experience in your industry. Make sure to have a personal meeting with any candidate before they become your legal counsel.

You must trust your lawyer. This individual will be privy to some of the most secret information of your business and must be able to handle this in a private and professional manner. It is a good idea to establish guidelines about the nature and sensitivity of company materials. Find out if there are any conflicts of interest that would make this individual the wrong person to handle your company.

You will want to find a lawyer who has experience dealing in the business world and is comfortable with contracts, licenses, copyrights, patents and other issues that will affect your business. Look for a lawyer who has had past dealings with similar yet non-competing companies, and will use his or her experience to help mitigate your exposure to unnecessary risk.

The best place to start your search for a lawyer is to speak with your friends and other business owners to find out who they use. You can also try looking in the Yellow Pages or on the Web. There are innumerable lawyers who will be able to handle the needs of your business from a professional standpoint. It is your job to find the one that will fit in best with your business team, understands the best ways to build a solid foundation for your business and can best cut down your risk exposure.

- What characteristics are you looking for in your legal counsel?

- Do you currently know any lawyers with experience in your industry?

- How will you give the lawyer a vested interest in the success of your business?

- Do you trust this individual?

- What do their references have to say about him or her?

- What is his or her familiarity with the industry?

- Do they have any other clients in the same industry?

Looking for a new challenge? The Vault Job Board has thousands of top jobs for all experience levels. Visit www.vault.com.

VAULT CAREER LIBRARY   113

Legal form of the business

The legal structure of your company is extremely important. The legal form of your business will have an effect on the amount you pay in taxes, your company and personal liability, investment capital and many other areas. Choosing the legal structure that best matches your company profile will help to ensure that your company experiences optimum protection and stability.

The basic options for the organization of your business are:

1. Sole proprietorship

Sole proprietorship is the simplest organizational structure to form. If you do not incorporate and do not have a partner, you are automatically a sole proprietorship. Operating a sole proprietorship means that the profit of your business is taxed as personal income, and you are personally liable for any debts or losses.

2. Incorporation

Incorporating provides your business with protection from liability. By incorporating, you are establishing your business as a legal entity separate from yourself. This means you and your personal assets are not liable if something goes wrong with the business.

3. S corporation

An S corporation provides you with the liability protection of a corporation and also enables you to pay taxes like a sole proprietor or partnership. Many experts recommend this for startups because it provides protection and reduces your tax burden.

4. C corporation

A C corporation allows your business to file and pay taxes on the income amount derived after all business expenses are deducted. It can be beneficial to establish a C corporation if you plan to keep large amounts of profits or other cash in the bank to make future capital expenditures. Unfortunately, entrepreneurs who set up C corporations are subject to potential double taxation – once as a corporation and a second time on a personal level when they cash in on the profits or sell the company.

5. Limited partnership

A limited partnership is generally used for real estate investments or when a business is planning financial expansion. The advantage of limited partnerships is they allow small businesses to raise capital without bringing in new partners, forming a corporation or issuing stock. Limited partners are not personally liable for the debts of the company and have the same tax rights as general partners, but usually cannot hold management positions.

6. Partnership

The benefit to forming a partnership is the ability to share the financial burden with another person or group of persons. Make sure to put the partnership agreement in writing. The risk of a partnership is that you are personally liable for the actions of the other partner(s).

7. Limited liability corporation

The limited liability corporation is a cross between a corporation and a partnership. It provides the beneficial tax breaks of a partnership while also offering the protection of a corporation. The LLC is very similar to the S Corporation and limited partnership but is more flexible.

8. Special cases

- *Non-Profit*
  The main benefit of being a non-profit is that you are exempt from paying income taxes. You must qualify under the IRS Section 501 (c)(3) rules. Typically, this designation is for organizations that are educational, scientific or religious in nature.

- *Professional Corporations*
  Professional corporations must be formed for the sole purpose of offering a professional service. They are usually formed to shield the owners from certain liabilities.

The descriptions listed above are very basic and do not include all of the intricacies of the different structures. They are meant to give you a basic idea of the different options available. Make sure to consult a legal professional and find out all of the benefits to the different organizational structures.

- Which aspects of incorporation are of the most benefit to your business?

- Which type of incorporation makes the most sense for your business?

- Do you have one or more potential partners, or will you bear sole responsibility?

- What tax and liability issues will affect your business?

- What structure best mitigates these issues?

Patents, copyrights, trademarks

A patent is a contract between the inventor of a product and the government. The inventor supplies the government with a detailed analysis and disclosure of all aspects of the invention. In return, the inventor receives exclusive rights to the invention for a specified amount of time. After the specified time has passed, the government will make the records public and available to everyone. It is important to make sure that you are not infringing on any one else's patent if you are designing a product.

There are three different types of patents. Utility patents are the most common; these are 17 years in length and begin on the date of issuance from the Patent and Trademark Office (PTO). A utility patent provides the inventor protection from other people using or profiting from the patented invention. Another type of patent, the design patent, protects new and original designs. These are valid for 14 years and give the inventor the exclusive right to use, sell, and profit from his or her invention. Plant patents are rare in nature and are issued for new varieties of manufacturing plants. They are issued for 17 years.

A patent application must contain everything associated with the design and production of the item you wish to have protected. It should contain an introduction section, a description of the invention, and direct claims of what makes your invention deserving of a patent. This should also be accompanied by a declaration of oath signed by the inventor. When applying for a patent, it is a good idea to have a patent lawyer guide you through the process. They will be able to make sure you fill out all of the necessary forms and present your information in such a way that you have the best chance of obtaining a patent.

A trademark is a word, design, symbol, slogan or combination thereof that identies a product or service with its source (the company). Trademarks, denoted with the symbol ™, provide notice to other businesses and individuals in the marketplace that you own the exclusive rights within the United States to the trademarked material. Registering entitles you to bring legal action against any party infringing on your trademarked material. Registered trademarks carry the symbol ® to identify them. It is important to know that you are not required to officially register your trademark on a national or state level. Previous use of a trademark denotes legal ownership. However, it is more secure to register your trademark on a national and state-by-state level to ensure protection. A trademark is ideal for a company that will be conducting business in several states and wants to protect the trademarked information on a national level. Trademarks are filed with the Patent and Trademark Office (PTO).

Copyrights protect original works of intellectual property, including written materials, music, art, and computer programs. Any material that is copyrighted is accompanied by the © symbol. What most people do not realize is that there is a much easier way to copyright your work that avoids the paperwork and fees associated with registering it with the federal government. If you simply attach the © symbol to your material, the law deems that you have made the appropriate notice of your piece of work. Copyrights usually can be obtained without the help of attorney. To register, you must fill out a Form TX, attach the fee and forward it to the Library of Congress for approval. The copyright is good for the life of the author plus fifty years. For institutions, the term of the copyright is seventy-five years from publication.

- Does your business own any material that should be registered for a trademark, copyright, or patent?

- How will filing protect your business?

- In what cases will you need the assistance of a lawyer?

Important documents

As you begin your business, there will be a number of important documents that will be responsible for shaping the legal framework of your business. In addition to the documents mentioned above, there are additional agreements that have the potential to seriously affect your business, such as contracts and licenses. By consulting a lawyer who can explain to you the significance of these documents, you will ensure that your business is not exposed to any

Looking for a new challenge? The Vault Job Board has thousands of top jobs for all experience levels. Visit www.vault.com.

VAULT CAREER LIBRARY **117**

unnecessary risk or liability. The change of even one word in these documents has the potential to seriously alter their legal meanings. Retaining a lawyer to help you look over these papers will not eliminate your risk entirely, but it will ensure that your business is not overly vulnerable.

Contracts are one type of document that are often extensive and require very specific wording to ensure their accuracy. In starting your business, you will sign contracts with landlords, clients, investors, partners and other individuals. Although some of these contracts may be very basic and will not involve large amounts of money, most will require examination by a lawyer. If you cannot afford a lawyer to look over the materials, make sure that the document is written in a way that you can understand and does not contain any opaque legal jargon. It is extremely important to have written contracts for all agreements made with another party.

The key elements of a contract are: having both parties sign the document, naming all individuals involved and their specific role, describing the exact dollar amount and structure of any financing and providing a detailed description of what constitutes fulfillment of the contract. Paying careful attention to these details will help to ensure that you have a binding contract with little room for misinterpretation.

Licenses are another document you should pay special attention to when starting your business. These are agreements whereby one of the participants is allowed to use some sort of proprietary information or technology that is owned by the other. For licensing the right to use this material, the licensee pays the licensor a royalty or fee. These agreements have particular appeal to holders of patents. It is an excellent way for them to leverage their patents and take advantage of resources unavailable to them individually. (Licenses are also frequently used with copyrighted and trademarked information.) Licensing is an excellent way for an entrepreneur to start a business without incurring extensive startup expenses.

Insurance, product safety, and liability are additional areas of legal concern for entrepreneurs. It is important to check if any components of your venture are subject to the Consumer Product Safety Act. The commission is responsible for setting safety standards for products and ensuring the overall safety of the general public. Claims made by consumers that fall under this act generally attract strict liability, negligence, warranty or misrepresentation attention.

• Which of the issues mentioned above apply to your business?

- What types of individuals will you need to consult for help?

- What contracts will be established with potential clients, customers, partners or investors?

Accounting/tax issues

Finding the right person(s) to handle the accounting and tax functions for your business will save you a lot of time, energy and hassle. Accurately estimating and reporting taxes, profit and loss statements, balance sheet items and cash flow analysis will help to stabilize the financial foundation of your business.

Looking for a new challenge? The Vault Job Board has thousands
of top jobs for all experience levels. Visit www.vault.com.

VAULT CAREER LIBRARY   119

General Legal Questions For Your Business

List of Information and Actions to be Completed in Connection with Incorporation

1. What will be the corporation's name?

2. What type of corporation is being formed?

3. What is the name and address of the registered agent?

4. Who is the incorporator(s) and his/her address?

5. If an S corporation is being formed, an application for recognition of S status (form 2553) will have to be filed before the 16th day of the 3rd month of the tax year in which the election is to take effect

Application for Employer Identification Number

1. Will the corporation be employing anyone? If so, when is the first employee expected to be hired?

2. When does the corporation's fiscal year end?

3. What will be the corporation's principal activity?

4. Will the corporation be selling goods to the public (retail), business (wholesale) or other? If other, what/where/who?

5. Has the corporation previously applied for a federal employer identification number? If not, form SS-4 will have to be filed, either via mail or telephone call with fax.

6. What is the Social Security Number of the officer who will be signing the SS-4?

Offices

1. Where will the main office be located?

2. Are there or will there be any branch offices?

Meetings

1. Where will the corporation hold its meetings of shareholders and directors?

2. When will annual shareholders' and directors' meetings be held?

Directors

1. How many directors will the corporation have?

2. Who will be the first directors?

Officers

1. How many officers will the corporation have?

2. Which offices will be provided? (President, Secretary, Treasurer)

3. Who will be the first officers?

Stock

1. How many shares of stock will be initially authorized? (Filing fee with the articles of incorporation automatically registers 60,000 shares; additional shares cost extra.)

2. How many of the authorized shares will actually be issued?

3. Who will the shares be issued to?

4. Will the shares have a par value? (Not necessary, but a common practice)

5. How many shares will be common or preferred?

Courtesy of:
Simon, Fakhoury, Tangalos & Frantz, PLC
355 East Big Beaver Road., Suite 211, Troy, MI 48083
Telephone: (248) 740-4800 Facsimile (248) 740-8400
E-mail: SFTF@voyager.net

Looking for a new challenge? The Vault Job Board has thousands
of top jobs for all experience levels. Visit www.vault.com.

VAULT CAREER LIBRARY   **121**

Special Entrepreneur Profiles

CHAPTER 8

Jay Levinson: Author, *Guerrilla Marketing*

Guerrilla Marketing is the act of achieving conventional goals, such as profits and joy, with unconventional methods, such as investing energy instead of money. The strategy and theory behind Guerrilla Marketing *was developed by Jay Conrad Levinson in 1984.* Guerrilla Marketing *focuses on providing businesses with marketing strategies that are simple to understand, easy to implement and inexpensive compared to traditional advertising methods.*

Jay writes a monthly column for Entrepreneur *magazine, articles for* Inc. *magazine, a syndicated column for newspapers and magazines and online columns published monthly on the Microsoft and GTE web sites. Jay has served on the Microsoft Small Business Council and the 3Com Small Business Advisory Board.*

Vault: How did you become involved in the *Guerrilla Marketing* book series and Guerrilla Marketing International?

JL: I was teaching a course in the late 1970's at the University of California Extension division, a course based upon my prior two books: *Earning Money Without a Job* and *555 Ways to Earn Extra Money*, both published by Henry Holt. When students asked for book recommendations about marketing, I couldn't find any books to fit their scant budgets. So I wrote *Guerrilla Marketing* as a service to my students. Little did I know it would take on a life of its own throughout the world, leading to many spin-offs and follow-up books. The speaking invitations that poured in after that book, along with my own desire to write a newsletter, spurred me to co-found Guerrilla Marketing International with Bill Shear. We now have several speakers, a CD-ROM, a video, several audio tapes, a killer web site and we also consult – so as to practice what we preach.

Vault: What led you to start Guerrilla Marketing Online?

JL: The growth of the Internet made it seem perfectly natural to include a site for *Guerrilla Marketing*. In addition, I co-authored the first of several *Guerrilla Marketing Online* books with Charles Rubin, so it would be silly to write that and not have a site as well. Today, that site is the lushest marketing site in all of cyberspace. I give credit for that to Bill Gallagher, Jr., son of the co-author of *Guerrilla Selling*. He runs that site on a full-time basis and keeps it very fresh.

Vault: What resources does it have to help entrepreneurs?

JL: It provides real-life guerrilla marketing tales, offers a daily marketing communiqué for $2.00 per year and also has columns of interest to entrepreneurs and a list of resources to help any entrepreneur with any type of marketing. The site is solely devoted to helping small and start-up businesses succeed by means of inexpensive and highly effective marketing.

Vault: What advice would you give someone starting their own business?

JL: I'd say to do everything on earth to avoid becoming a workaholic. And I'd recommend that any business started should be one about which the business owner feels true passion. The other requisites for success are determination, discipline, a high sense of organization and a love of life beyond business – so that you maintain balance in your life. Life comes first and business comes next.

Vault: What other resources would you recommend for entrepreneurs and small business owners?

JL: I think I've put every single resource into that web site. Mostly, I'd recommend my own *The Way of the Guerrilla* because it will help entrepreneurs get off on the right foot. I'd also recommend regular visits to sites such as Microsoft.com/smallbiz and ltbn.com (Let's Talk Business Network).

Vault: What is the main message you are trying to get across to entrepreneurs?

JL: The main messages in my books are to strive for freedom and balance and then to aim for success in business. I also want readers to realize that advertising is only one percent of marketing and that it does not cost nearly as much to market as many people think.

Larry Downes: Co-author, *Unleashing the Killer App*

Unleashing the Killer App, written by Larry Downes and Chunka Mui, is a book that explains the effects of digital strategy on transforming the marketplace. Digital strategy focuses on a new approach of planning and strategy that is better suited to plummeting technology prices, exploding networks, and "marketplaces" with fewer transaction costs. By-products of the digital strategy include "killer apps," applications that have the ability to transform industries, unseat market leaders, and provide a thousandfold return on an initial investment. The main principle of the book is that technology is no longer the solution, but the problem. Larry Downes tells us about job-hopping, and how he thinks businesses can "unleash the killer app."

Vault: Tell me a little about your backgrounds.

LD: I have had several careers, I'm afraid to say. I actually majored in English and History in college, but rather than go directly to grad school I decided to work a few years to pay off some debt. I was lucky enough to graduate at the end of the 1970s, when consulting firms were growing so fast that they were even willing to hire liberal arts majors, and I got a job with Andersen Consulting (then Arthur Andersen & Co.).

Of course I never went back to grad school, or anyway not in English or History. I was fortunate to have eight years off and on doing large-scale systems work with Andersen, then joined a very ill-conceived start-up firm called The Information Consulting Group, which was funded by the even more ill-conceived Saatchi & Saatchi consulting operation. After a year of that, we merged with McKinsey, and I stayed there for a while working on the systems end of strategy projects. I decided I needed a break from consulting, and ten years out of college decided to go to law school at the University of Chicago. After law school I had the singular privilege of clerking for a year with Chief Judge Richard A. Posner of the U.S. Court of Appeals in Chicago, and then practiced law very briefly in Silicon Valley before returning to consulting, first with CSC Index and then on my own. In addition to writing and speaking, I now consult on digital strategy projects in association with Diamond Technology Partners and teach at Northwestern University.

Looking for a new challenge? The Vault Job Board has thousands of top jobs for all experience levels. Visit www.vault.com.

VAULT CAREER LIBRARY   125

Chunka's background is a little more traditional. He graduated from MIT, where he had worked in the Artificial Intelligence lab, and joined Andersen a few years after I did to help develop Andersen's [artificial intelligence] practice in the mid-1980s. He moved on to do advanced software engineering research with Andersen, in part under government contract, and then joined CSC Index, where he worked on large re-engineering projects before starting the Vanguard research program (which we describe in the preface of the book).

A year and a half ago, he joined Diamond Technology Partners, where he directs the Exchange, an interdisciplinary program that brings senior executives together with leading strategy and technology developers several times a year. He is also Executive Editor of *Context*, a new business journal that addresses the impact of technology on new strategy. He and I rotate on a quarterly column called "Technosynthesis" which explores developments since we finished writing the book.

Vault: Tell me a little bit about why you both decided to write *Unleashing the Killer App*.

LD: From different perspectives, Chunka and I became convinced that our strategy work was heading in the wrong direction. I was frustrated by the lateness with which technology entered the process on McKinsey projects, and Chunka had come to see that re-engineering efforts were missing really dramatic, explosive outside developments that were reducing the effectiveness of these cost-cutting projects. Even before we began working together for the second time at CSC Index, we had begun a running dialog on the potential impact of the Internet (this was before there was a World Wide Web). Chunka convinced me that it really did have the potential to disrupt not only the cherished proprietary architecture strategies of the computing and communications giants but the structure of a growing list of non-technology industries.

After a few years of this conversation and several prototype projects with forward-thinking clients, we decided we had something worth writing about and began our research in earnest.

Vault: What are the principles behind the book?

LD: The main principle of the book is that technology is no longer the solution, but the problem. All of our clients in every industry have traditionally seen digital technology as the way to implement various strategic and operational initiatives, with varying degrees of success. Our strong belief is that this approach must be turned on its head. Strategy must now begin by understanding that it is digital technology itself which is the chief source of competitive threat, aided by its sister forces: deregulation and globalization.

Planning, consequently, becomes a much faster activity, based less on detailed quantitative analysis of current trends and more on the development of many, possibly contradictory, scenarios of how customers, markets and competitors will change over a shorter time. It must include not just senior executives but line managers as well, and it must be developed, not with reports and slide presentations, but with prototypes and experiments that prove or disprove the different scenarios. The notion of controlling an organization's future is long dead; the best today's business leaders can hope for is to ride the right waves. For some, that's a more interesting way to operate anyway. For others, well, remember the old Chinese curse, "May you live in interesting times." We will be living in interesting times, thanks to the remarkable science that is behind computing and communications, for some time to come.

To respond to these new forces, we have developed an approach we call "digital strategy," because it leads with technology and, more importantly, takes into account the very different way that planning must be done in order to unleash killer apps. We present an organized set of the twelve most important design principles (such as 'Outsource to the customer' and 'Treat your assets as liabilities') that successful companies have internalized as they change not only themselves but their entire industries. And we try to make it all real by providing detailed examples of the strategies in practice, as well as some real-world stories of some of our clients and how they got started with the process.

Vault: What killer apps do you feel are emerging today in the marketplace?

LD: To us, killer apps are no longer computer products and services per se, but the interesting combinations that innovative business leaders are creating in their own industries. In the securities industry, for example, it's already clear (except to a few ostrich-like firms with heads firmly and deeply in sand) that the Internet provides a superior channel for the full range of trading activities, including research, portfolio management, trading and even the

Looking for a new challenge? The Vault Job Board has thousands of top jobs for all experience levels. Visit www.vault.com.

VAULT CAREER LIBRARY   127

structuring of financial deals. Look at how firms like Schwab, E*Trade, Wit Capital and others are tinkering with the very core of what had been a pretty stable market, taking advantage of the information and technology infrastructure of the Internet to throw all assumptions about how one makes money in that industry into the garbage.

The same thing is happening in banking, retailing (including not just books and CDs but cars, white goods and even groceries), business-to-business trade, manufacturing, distribution, government, you name it. Look at how organizations like the University of Phoenix are changing even the very mature (or so it was thought) market for higher education. By comparison, most American universities look and act positively medieval in their attitude toward their customers and their products and services.

What makes any of these innovations "killer" apps is the way in which they happen right under the noses of the established, powerful, highly-financed players who ought to be – and could be – doing the innovations themselves. Stock brokers and booksellers now see that they've missed the boat, and we believe that it is only a matter of time before car dealers, travel agents, insurance companies and entertainment firms (to name a few) will likewise rue the day they dismissed these experiments as toys.

Vault: What do you feel was the most challenging part of writing the book?

LD: Keeping it current! One of the hardest features of today's business environment is the accelerating speed at which it is changing. Our research became outdated with great speed, and we were adding examples that didn't exist when we started right up until the moment of publication. Of course, once the book went into production we couldn't do that anymore, and the result was that when it actually hit the stands some months later, we felt there was a great deal of new material we wanted to share with our readers. This is why we have invested heavily in the creation of our web site, www.killer-apps.com. Our hope is to use it not just to advertise the book but to continue the process of writing it. More importantly, it gives us a chance to experiment with having a two-way conversation with our readers, something we would dearly have loved to do while we were writing.

Vault: What did you find was the most rewarding aspect?

LD: We've both been very encouraged by the positive feedback we've received from our outside and inside reviewers (Harvard put the manuscript through an extensive peer review process) and readers, who come from a remarkable range of backgrounds, from business students in Australia to the presidents of major corporations. In particular, we have heard from a number of people who say that they share our belief about the need to change the way planning and strategy are performed, but haven't had a mechanism for spreading that message inside their own organization. We're hoping that the book and the web site gives the entrepreneur hiding inside every organization the ammunition to change the attitude of his or her peers – or to leave and do it on their own.

Vault: How do you see your conclusions affecting entrepreneurs?

LD: We believe that the only successful businesspeople in today's and tomorrow's environments will be entrepreneurs, whether literally individuals starting businesses on their own or inside existing organizations (our colleagues Gordon Bell and Heidi Mason call such folk "intrapreneurs"). The spirit and discipline of entrepreneurs, like those in Silicon Valley who are making the technology revolution, are exactly what is necessary to succeed at digital strategy.

Vault: How does your book help entrepreneurs who are thinking of starting their own business?

LD: Since many of the design principles we provide came from start-up businesses, we have no doubt that the techniques and the rules of digital strategy are just as useful to entrepreneurs as they are to global business executives, perhaps even more so. And entrepreneurs have at least one advantage over their corporate counterparts: they don't have a legacy of old thinking and old technology to overcome.

Vault: What advice would you give an entrepreneur starting their own business?

LD: These are exciting times for entrepreneurs, with many opportunities and rapidly-falling barriers to entering markets and trying new business models. Much of what we know we have learned from entrepreneurs, and we

Looking for a new challenge? The Vault Job Board has thousands
of top jobs for all experience levels. Visit www.vault.com.

VAULT CAREER LIBRARY   **129**

encourage those considering the start of a new business to talk to people who have already done it and learn from their successes and failures.

Some of the old rules still apply, however. We have seen many – too many – new ventures (some financed with millions of dollars of venture capital, some with the family nest egg) fail, not because of a bad idea but because of poor business skills. No matter how small your organization, you need some basic infrastructure, systems and business discipline to make it work. Spend your money carefully and keep track of where it's going. Work hard, be honest with yourself (and with everyone with whom you deal,) and make sure you've got enough capital to go twice as long as you think it will take to start making money.

Above all, have fun. That's where the great ideas – and the killer apps – come from.

Walter J. Aspatore: Founding Partner, Amherst Capital Partners

Amherst Capital Partners provides investment banking and financial advisory services to middle market and small companies located primarily in the Midwest, although it also has clients elsewhere in the country and internationally. Lending its abilities to a wide range of areas, the firm currently services clients in the manufacturing, distribution, telecommunications, high technology, health care, retail and financial industries. Founding partner Walter Aspatore talks about finding a niche market in the big bad world of investment banking.

Vault: How did you get interested in starting your own business?

WA: After the sale of our publicly-traded company, Cross and Trecker Corp., Chrysler Corp. approached me about providing me an equity stake in a small investment fund in which they were the largest investor. This fund invested in small- to medium-sized businesses that had strong technological underpinnings and good growth opportunities. A number of these firms asked us to provide additional services more closely associated with traditional merger and acquisition services. Because the fund's objective was to be an equity or debt participant, we could not provide the desired additional services. With the Chrysler debt restructuring of the mid-1990s, the fund shut down. In 1994, we established Amherst Capital specifically to satisfy M&A and financial advisory services needs.

Vault: Is this something you always planned on doing? Had you started a business before?

WA: This opportunity came about as a direct result of identifying a marketplace need, as opposed to a long-desired plan to start a business. After many years of working for large publicly held corporations, Bendix, TRW, Allied Signal and Cross and Trecker, we decided to start Amherst.

Vault: What do you feel is the most challenging aspect of starting and owning your own business?

WA: The most challenging aspect of starting and owning Amherst has been the initial need to develop clients, to fund payroll for our employees while

Looking for a new challenge? The Vault Job Board has thousands
of top jobs for all experience levels. Visit www.vault.com.

VAULT CAREER LIBRARY   **131**

simultaneously completing client engagements. Since its inception four years ago, Amherst has had over 100 clients.

Vault: What do you find is the most rewarding aspect?

WA: The most rewarding aspect is the confirmation of providing value enhancement to our clients, the referrals of various business professionals and follow up on engagements from previously served clients.

Vault: Where do you see your business going in the future?

WA: The future of this business will, to some degree, ebb and flow with the economy. However, as we become more established and large investment banking houses merge or are acquired by banks, we will continue to pursue our niche strategy. This should help solidify our position with small to medium sized companies.

Vault: How do you plan to grow your business?

WA: We will stick to our basic strategy of servicing the small to medium-sized companies. Due to the various mergers and acquisitions of various local investment banking acquisitions, Amherst will be positioned to fill the void at the lower end of the transaction range.

Vault: What interests you about what you are doing?

WA: Simple: the feeling of accomplishment when our assignment is completed and the client feels we have contributed to increased shareholder value. In addition, working across various industries and assignments provides a seemingly endless variety of opportunities and challenges without ever becoming boring.

Vault: What resources were helpful to you when starting your business?

WA: The most helpful resources available when we started were the many years of experience working in varied industries, with people from all across the world and at all levels of these organizations from the Board of Directors to the CEO on down. Also extremely helpful were the years of personal contacts we had developed. In the beginning, as it is today, our personal experiences and relationships provide the foundation of our business.

Vault: How have you used your business to open other doors for yourself?

WA: The successful completion of a transaction or enhancing shareholder value provides a multiplier effect. The more successful we are, the more in demand we become. Professionals, be they accountants, lawyers, bankers or other business owners, only want to be associated with people or organizations they perceive as winners. If they refer you to one of their clients or acquaintances and you do a good job, this reflects well on them. Unfortunately, the opposite is also true.

Vault: What advice would you give someone else starting their own business?

WA: Seek role models. Learn from their successes and failures. Be diligent in your pursuit of knowledge. Take the time to do the work. If you don't know something, don't be afraid to admit it. You can't fool people. If they think you are BSing, you have lost. On the other hand, most people have a genuine desire to help other individuals, but only when they feel someone is sincere. Find professionals to help you. Accountants, lawyers, bankers, other business people. They want to help. The best thing someone can know is what they don't know. People will help. Go out of your way to schmooze with other people. Schmoozing is a never-ending process. Help those that need help just as others helped you. Remember, what goes around, comes around!

Vault: What are your general thoughts on entrepreneurship?

WA: Work hard. Respect others. Learn to get along with everyone. Never quit learning. Seek advice from others. Plan, plan, plan. Serendipity is great, but rare; make your own breaks, be positive, work smart, use common sense and above all else – be known for your integrity.

Looking for a new challenge? The Vault Job Board has thousands
of top jobs for all experience levels. Visit www.vault.com.

V/\ULT CAREER LIBRARY   **133**

Sam Simon: President & CEO, Atlas Oil Company

Husband-and-wife team Nada and Sam Simon, Armenian immigrants, came to the United States 23 years ago in search of opportunities. Today, their Southfield, Michigan-based petroleum wholesale company, Atlas Oil has more than 150 employees and suppliers from nearly every major oil company. Nada is a member of the Atlas Oil sales team. President and CEO Sam discusses building a $140 million business with an idea and a couple of credit cards.

Vault: Tell me a little about how you started Atlas Oil.

SS: Atlas Oil was formed in October 1985. Atlas was started by Shell Oil Company, who wanted diesel fuel in the local area for their trucks. I designed a way to provide this to them and received a commission. I then went on to buy my own gas truck, using my Visa and Mastercard to make the payments. I did not want to ask my father for money so I paid the 18 percent on the balances until they were all paid off. Twenty-three years later, the company has grown to $140 million in sales and over 150 employees.

Vault: What were some of the challenges of starting your own business?

SS: Starting Atlas Oil required a lot of hard work and desire. Starting a business can be very difficult because you are competing against established businesses. Therefore, you have to find your niche and perform to a higher standard.

Vault: What have you found to be some of the rewards of entrepreneurship?

SS: Atlas Oil focuses on offering the best quality and service. Our success is measured by the quality we provide to our customers. It is also very rewarding to see our company grow. Going from four employees to over 150, it is amazing to see the hard work pay off for myself and other individuals at the company. We are currently planning on expanding to other states and capitalizing on new business ventures within the retail station marketplace.

Vault: What have been the keys to the success of Atlas Oil?

SS: By continuing to provide the highest level of quality and service to our customers, we plan to succeed in marketplaces nationwide. The key to Atlas Oil has been to bring quality individuals into to our business. Our goal is to have the highest quality employees to create the most value for our business. Customers realize that Atlas stands for quality and want to do business with us.

Vault: What are your general feelings on entrepreneurship?

SS: My feeling is that entrepreneurship is not for everyone. Being an entrepreneur requires a lot of skills and behavioral aspects that cannot be learned. For me, it is the challenge that I love. When someone tells me that I cannot do something, I always find a way to prove them wrong. Money is not everything. Seeing an opportunity in the marketplace and then finding a way to capitalize is the rewarding part. When I see an opportunity I have to take advantage of it. Learning to work hard really prepared me to start my own business. I learned from seeing how hard my dad worked and what he did to survive and prosper when moving to the United States with no money. As a family, we learned to work very hard and do what it took to succeed.

Vault: What advice would you give to other entrepreneurs starting their own business?

SS: When starting your own business, you have to give it all you have. Success is definitely attainable if you are persistent and believe in yourself. The sacrifices that you have to make in the beginning are well worth it when your business succeeds. Stay strong and believe in yourself and the quality of your company.

Looking for a new challenge? The Vault Job Board has thousands of top jobs for all experience levels. Visit www.vault.com.

VAULT CAREER LIBRARY 135

Sam Kinney: EVP and Co-founder, FreeMarkets Online

FreeMarkets OnLine enables large industrial buyers to save substantial amounts of money by creating efficient online markets for the purchase of a variety of industrial parts such as plastic molded parts, metal-machined parts, and electronic components. The company is the world's first online industrial market maker for custom industrial products. Using its BidWare® software, FreeMarkets enables suppliers to submit bids in an interactive marketplace to compete for business.

Founded in 1995, the Pittsburgh-based company has maintained an annual revenue growth rate of close to 400 percent. Located in downtown Pittsburgh, the company has grown to more than 1,000 employees as of 2001 and features some of the world's largest companies as clients. Co-founder Sam Kinney talks about managing explosive growth.

Vault: Tell me a little about your background.

SK: I have five years of general management consulting experience with the big-name firms (two years with Booz Allen, three years with McKinsey). A friend of mine once described spending time in management consulting as "getting your PhD in business." This is an apt characterization – intense learning curve, dealing with senior executive issues and senior executive communications challenges. In addition, I was a division budget director for an aerospace manufacturing concern for two years, where I learned the "guts" of a manufacturing environment inside and out.

Vault: Tell me a little bit about your business.

SK: FreeMarkets OnLine is the world's first online industrial market maker. We have combined under one roof a number of different competencies and glued them together with technology and innovative pricing. On behalf of industrial buyers who purchase custom components to assemble into their product, we create custom spot markets where potential suppliers of those components submit bids electronically in a downward-price auction. In doing this, we are creating a true "market price" for items where a market price is not ordinarily available, because the components are often custom-made to the buyer's blueprint.

In some ways, we repackage steps already done in buying and selling under one roof – a reengineering of the sales process. But then we enhance it with depth of knowledge and technology.

Vault: How did you get interested in starting your own business?

SK: I've always known I needed to start my own business. I long ago discovered that my "highest and best use" as a business person was more or less in "business R&D" – the business building process of planning, prototyping, visioning, networking with people, etc. I am pretty bad at doing the same thing a second or third time – so I needed a role where I could be inventing every day.

It's hard to find a role like that in a traditional organization, so I needed to break out and define an organization around that role. I also needed a partner like Glen Meahem who was the opposite – driven and detail- oriented. You might call my role a necessary but insufficient piece of starting the business.

Vault: Is this something you always planned on doing?

SK: Pretty much, yes. I always knew I would, but definitely needed to work until my confidence level was high and I had enough of the "vocational" experiences under my belt. For me, the right time came when I had enough consulting experience that in a business failure scenario, I knew I had a fallback position with some earning power.

Vault: What do you feel is the most challenging aspect of starting and owning your own business?

SK: Making tradeoffs in the face of unlimited opportunities/demands and limited resources. We've had a pretty good strategic gut for where to go, and so far haven't strayed too far.

High technology is a funny market. The technology itself comes and goes so quickly that it's always dynamic. And it is subject to many "flavor of the month fads," particularly in the Internet space. Everybody seems to get caught up in these moves, including the venture capitalists. So while technology is on the one hand very innovative, there seems to be a fast-changing conventional wisdom that is behind everybody's decision making. We've largely been contrarians in this regard, choosing to locate in Pittsburgh and away from much of that hype. We've clearly set our own direction pretty

Looking for a new challenge? The Vault Job Board has thousands
of top jobs for all experience levels. Visit www.vault.com.

VAULT CAREER LIBRARY   **137**

much without regard to the fads of the month. In just the last two years, for example, we've seen the emergence and rapid death of fads like "multimedia," Java, push technology, network convergence and Internet malls. All of these "trends" were highly touted by the "experts" at their emergence.

We've taken a much more conservative approach – building the right service that clients will pay for, and growing the business as paying clients will allow. But you have to be resolute in that strategy, since there are always hundreds of "experts" telling us that "nobody else does it that way."

Vault: What do you find is the most rewarding aspect?

SK: Finding untapped young talent and creating a culture that unleashes their energies. I find nothing more thrilling than to see a person grow in their career at a rapid pace, especially when we "took a bet" on that person and hired them with little direct experience in what we have them doing now.

Vault: How do you plan to grow your business?

SK: The growth challenge has more to do with organizational structure and culture now than with market demand. The demand is there. It comes in a variety of forms, as you might expect for a custom business service. So the organization has to be adaptable.

The primary concern, however, is how do we 1) give our people growth and responsibility and financial reward opportunities, while 2) maintaining flexible and excellent client service. Conceptually, our growth probably has to look like that at GE Capital, a phenomenal growth and profit engine. They have some big powerful core businesses, but are terrific at spawning smaller profit centers which collectively add up to big dollars. They are the best financial training ground in the world too, so they've done it in a professionally rewarding way. We're just getting to the critical mass of people and financial strength where we can start to plant growth seeds in this way.

Vault: What interests you about what you are doing?

SK: As an economist, I am fascinated by market efficiency and the economist Joseph Schumpeter's doctrine of "creative destruction." All around us are markets of varying degrees of efficiency. The U.S. stock markets are famously efficient. The market for industrial components is terribly inefficient. Markets get efficient over noticeably short time frames. In the last 15 years, home mortgages have become complete commodities due to the opening of capital markets for trading mortgages. We are doing the same for industrial products.

The creative destruction piece is very evident. Many businesses that sell product and are viable, would not be economically fit to survive a more efficient marketplace. Their protected niches go away as information becomes more available to professional purchasers like us. So we are hastening the consolidation and restructuring of markets. We've seen plant closures as a result of market outcomes in our markets, as a more efficient source of supply is substituted for a less efficient one. While that is a terribly painful occurrence for a company when faced with that, the source of the problem is really just the market forces. We just happen to be wielding those market forces. You have to be somewhat Darwinian to appreciate this.

Vault: What resources were helpful to you when starting your business?

SK: The single most important factor is having the right team. I was incredibly fortunate Glen wanted me on this team. Frankly, the next most important set of resources were the accumulated personal and professional network each of the early team members brought. That network ultimately provided capital, clients, encouragement, and more employees.

We've had an interesting time starting the business in Pittsburgh. Pittsburgh has a deserved reputation for being insular. On a purely demographic basis, there is not much transient flow of people to and from Pittsburgh. One result of this is that local entrepreneurs start and stop their search for business resources here. Because we are not natives, and our networks were built on the business schools and consulting firms of our background, we have always leaned on a national and even international network. Our first investor group came from 13 states and three countries.

Vault: What advice would you give someone else starting their own business?

SK: Starting a business is the culmination of a lifetime of preparation. In our case, Glen and I had spent our early careers in various stages of explicit or implicit preparation. You mull over ideas. You examine businesses that succeed and look for the underlying insights leading to their success. You figure out what kind of industry or function you enjoy. I would call this the gestation of the ideas. Entrepreneurs are of course full of ideas, most of

Looking for a new challenge? The Vault Job Board has thousands
of top jobs for all experience levels. Visit www.vault.com.

VAULT CAREER LIBRARY **139**

which don't amount to anything. Only a few are really good enough to bet your financial future on.

Then there are the skills. You have to spend enough time learning the "vocational" skills of business building. In our case, this included items like preparing a financial plan, writing a marketing brochure, presenting to a senior client audience, and even as mundane as designing the chart of accounts for the accounting system. Despite what many say, the classical MBA curriculum is a huge benefit. There is no question that the more of this tactical stuff you can dispatch with ease, the better your business launch will be.

Finally, the very implicit stuff comes down to leaving a stellar track record of achievement. When you start raising capital for a business, your references will be scrutinized like never before, so your reference contacts must be ready to gush on your behalf. Your credit history will be pulled dozens of times, so it better look pretty good. Past associates and managers are a source of capital. In my case, these past associates "knew the call would be coming some day" because they "knew" that someday, I would be starting a business. You have to leave a track record like that, where people want to back your idea no matter how off-the wall.

Vault: What are your general thoughts on entrepreneurship?

SK: Find the right partner. Use the "discovery based planning" method – establish your assumptions, then methodically prove or disprove these assumptions, starting with the highest risk assumptions first. Leave nothing to chance.

Russell Zack: President, i33

Conceived and created in 1993 by Russell Zack, William Tigertt III, Jani Anderson, and Rodrigo Sanchez, i33 is Detroit's largest independently-owned interactive design studio, specializing in a complete range of innovative web page design services and interactive marketing strategies. Headquartered in downtown Detroit's historic Harmonie Park, i33 has done projects for companies such as Ford, GMC Truck, Cadillac, Delphi, and Sun Microsystems. Since its humble beginnings nine years ago with only $5,000 in capital, i33 has received numerous industry awards for excellence in the field of web page design, including the coveted Triomphe Award at the recent International Awards Ceremony for its work with GMC. i33 is now comprised of 32 employees (average age 26) with offices in New York and Detroit. Co-founder Russell Zack talks about being called crazy for creating his own major in college and starting a successful business.

Vault: Tell me a little about your background.

RZ: I'm originally from Montreal, Quebec. My parents have been involved with two different sides of technology for the past 30 years. My mother does research for the Canadian government. Her doctoral thesis was an analysis of children's approaches to using computers as a learning tool. It was based, I believe, on a program called Logo developed at MIT – one of the first programs of its kind to try to take simple graphics and creativity and marry it with math. She used my twin brother and I as guinea pigs before she found real students for the thesis.

My father initially worked at IBM, then was the MIS director at Wonder Bra. He left Wonder Bra about thirty years ago to start his own company, STS Systems, which develops information technology systems for the retail industry, especially apparel. The software, hardware and services STS offers cover the entire spectrum of a large retail merchandiser's supply chain. The company is still privately held with 650 employees and six offices.

I came to the United States after being accepted at the University of Michigan. Admittedly, I made the decision to attend an American school rather late in the game – after I 'd become frustrated with the level of innovation and technology at Canadian schools. Having never prepared for the SAT, I prepared in a week, took the test, then applied to Northwestern, the

Looking for a new challenge? The Vault Job Board has thousands of top jobs for all experience levels. Visit www.vault.com.

VAULT CAREER LIBRARY   **141**

University of Chicago and U of M. I finally chose the University of Michigan because of its diversity and the strength of its undergraduate BBA program.

Vault: Tell me a little bit about your business.

RZ: i33 is an interactive media agency. We are part strategic consultant, part systems integrator, and part advertising agency. Our business is completely focused on "interactive media," a general term used to describe multimedia (text, graphics and sound) digital technologies that are used to present, manage and transact information. The nature of our expertise is in helping large companies plan, produce, and promote their products and services using these technologies. Basically, it's a mixture of interactive strategy, marketing and technology.

Vault: How did you get interested in starting your own business?

RZ: I've always wanted to run my own company. I guess it's a merging of both nature and nurture. I remember thinking about it for the first time when I was in fifth grade. We had to put down a job description of what we wanted to do when we were older because we had a "Career Shadowing" day scheduled. We were basically going to watch someone work for a day. A lot of people put down fun stuff like a radio disk jockey or TV reporter and got these great days. I put down CEO of a large company and ended up with an insurance salesman for the day. Boy, was that disappointing…

I became truly engrossed in interactive media while I was attending college. But it goes back even slightly farther than that; the summer before I started at U of M, I read a book put out by Phaidon Press called *Introduction to Hypermedia*. It was a book that profoundly changed the way I thought about the interaction between people and information. Once I arrived at U of M, my friends thought I was crazy for passing on an acceptance to the business school in order to create my own major – a major that was the first of its kind to concentrate on "Digital Multimedia." I knew then that this was truly an industry for me. Before graduating I eventually met up with the people who would become my partners. Even in the early stages of collaborating with them, I knew the four of us had something truly special in the way in which we were able to work together.

Vault: What do you feel is the most challenging aspect of starting and owning your own business?

RZ: Proving yourself, both as a company on the whole and with your partners. I think that chemistry between partners is one of the most important things. It can't be forced and requires a lot of give and take between yourself and the people you're working with. It's much like a marriage of sorts, with concessions on every side.

I also think that access to the proper growing capital is essential. Making sure that the bottom line is met is obviously a challenge and a necessity to the success of any business, but squeezing to make ends meet all the time can cause business owners to miss the big picture. At the same time, especially in our business, I've seen companies with access to too much capital fall apart, where being a bit tighter as an enterprise may have kept them together.

Vault: What do you find is the most rewarding aspect?

RZ: My love for what I do. I think I'm fortunate to be so passionate about my lifestyle and profession. I honestly do believe that today's revolution in the way that companies do business will only be here once in my lifetime. I'm glad to be a part of that revolution and to be right at the tip of the wave. The view is great.

Vault: Where do you see the future of your business going?

RZ: A tough question. Our industry has changed so radically over the last couple of years. It's hard to put a five-year plan in place because of the speed inherent to technological change. But any successful business in our industry needs revision, revision, revision. I see us as a premium services driven company, as a mix of Andersen Consulting, EDS, and McCann-Erickson. We are an example of a new type of company that can expand and contract at will based on the needs of our clients. But we also keep a close eye on technology change and innovation as well as opportunities, funding and refunding our portfolio of internal projects or small garage companies in a way that keeps us on the cutting edge.

Vault: What interests you about what you are doing?

RZ: The constant innovation. The constant change. If we don't stay on top on what we're doing, our competitors will pass us by, not walking, but running. This is not a challenge we face monthly but daily. It's a challenge that keeps me hungry. The evolving nature of enabling technology keeps me excited.

Looking for a new challenge? The Vault Job Board has thousands of top jobs for all experience levels. Visit www.vault.com.

VAULT CAREER LIBRARY   **143**

Vault: What resources were helpful to you when starting your business?

RZ: In terms of people, I have to say my father, my mother, a mentor at the University of Michigan, and the advice of my twin brother. For information – constant reading, books, publications, browsing the Web.

Vault: How have you used your business to open other doors for yourself?

RZ: I find it's been an amazing opportunity in terms of learning how other businesses work. Since we deal with so many different companies by helping them develop digital strategy, I have been in the position to truly see how digital technologies are influencing a wide variety of industries. Presently, we do a lot of automotive work, and it makes things especially interesting to see how the product that is the gem of the Industrial Revolution is being affected by the Information Revolution.

Vault: What advice would you give someone else starting their own business?

RZ: Understand your business. If it's only about making money, quit now. No truly great entrepreneur was in it because of the money. It's about passion and challenge. Understand that you are going to have to make sacrifices. Forget about the best of both worlds; you have only one. Make sure that you surround yourself with people you trust and who trust you.

Vault: What are your general thoughts on entrepreneurship?

RZ: There's no better time than right now. Watching – as well as participating in – the rise and fall of hundreds of new companies during the emergence of the New Economy will be something wonderful to look back upon. Something I'll be proud to have been a participant in.

Also, for me, the challenges of entrepreneurship are rewarding enough – even without the guarantees of monetary reward. Although no can ever fully determine the future of their business, the gamble and the ability to control your professional destiny become their own rewards.

Appendix

Sample Business Plan

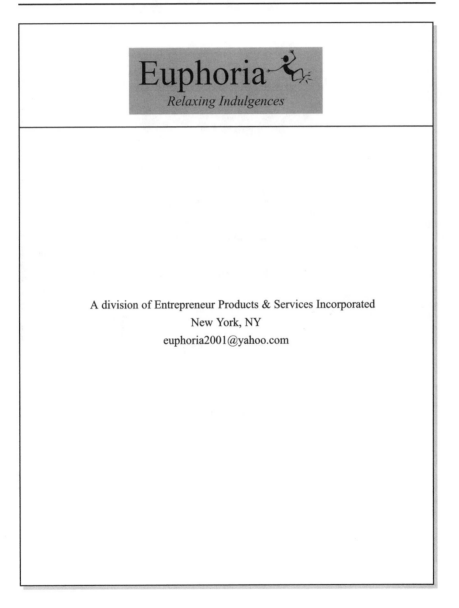

A division of Entrepreneur Products & Services Incorporated

New York, NY

euphoria2001@yahoo.com

Looking for a new challenge? The Vault Job Board has thousands
of top jobs for all experience levels. Visit www.vault.com.

VAULT CAREER LIBRARY   145

Euphoria

Relaxing Indulgences

TABLE OF CONTENTS

Introduction

Executive Summary

Industry Analysis

Description of Venture

Merchandising Plan

Marketing Plan

Organizational Plan

Assessment of Risk

Financial Plan

Euphoria

Relaxing Indulgences

Owner: Jennifer Pirone

Description of Business:
Euphoria will be a place where individuals can get an affordable massage in a very plush and cozy atmosphere. The stores will be located in highly trafficked, trendy areas which attract business professionals, shoppers and other pedestrians. In addition, high-quality lines of aromatherapy and skin care products will be sold. Euphoria plans to expand rapidly to gain a large share of the rapidly growing massage marketplace.

Financing:
Initial financing requested is $75,000, representing costs associated with opening the first store (proof of concept). Additional financing of $300,000 will be requested for the opening of four stores later the same year. This equity will cover retail space, advertising, salary, store equipment/furniture and remaining start-up costs for the first store.

This report is confidential and is the property of the owner listed above. It is intended only for use by the person to whom it is transmitted and any reproduction or divulgence of any of its contents without the prior written consent of the company is prohibited.

Looking for a new challenge? The Vault Job Board has thousands of top jobs for all experience levels. Visit www.vault.com.

VAULT CAREER LIBRARY **147**

Euphoria
Relaxing Indulgences

EXECUTIVE SUMMARY

Concept
A fashionable and affordable place to get a massage and purchase high-quality aromatherapy and skin care products in a trendy and populated area.

Industry Focus
Massages have become increasingly popular. The only business providing them now is The Great American Back Rub (in addition to expensive spas) which has bland decor and less-than-affordable rates. Women are always looking for new skin care and aromatherapy products, and an increasing number of men are buying these products as well. Euphoria plans to create a very fashionable and cozy atmosphere while offering innovative and new skin care and aromatherapy products.

Competition: Spas, Great American Back Rub

Location: First Store – New York City

Profits: Massages, Aromatherapy & Skin Care Products

Future
Additional stores in Manhattan, subsequent expansion to Boston, San Francisco and other major cities. Focus will remain in working districts inhabited by both businesses and tourist attractions.

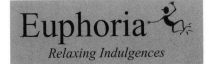

Euphoria
Relaxing Indulgences

Executive Summary, cont'd

Start-up Funds:	Approximately $75,000
12 Mo. Projections:	$1/3$ Capacity ($48,607)
	$1/2$ Capacity $65,155
	$3/4$ Capacity $235,793

Looking for a new challenge? The Vault Job Board has thousands
of top jobs for all experience levels. Visit www.vault.com.

VAULT CAREER LIBRARY   **149**

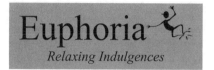

INDUSTRY ANALYSIS

The massage market is a hot industry. As individuals continue working longer hours, taking fewer vacations and becoming accustomed to stressful lifestyles, they will seek more relaxing indulgences. Euphoria is designed to help these individuals escape from reality for a brief amount of time and visit our "mini spa" for a relaxing indulgence. In addition, they will be able to purchase aromatherapy and skin care products. The market for these items has grown dramatically over the last three years. Top manufacturers of these products, such as Caswell & Massey, Burt's Bees and Votive, have enjoyed unprecedented success in the marketplace.

One of the main reasons the massage market is so attractive is because the monthly overhead is so low. Little inventory will be kept and every massage administered is almost 100 percent profit. The number of applicants to massage institutes, such as The Swedish Institute in New York, has risen dramatically in the last two years.

By creating a very comfortable and posh environment, keeping overhead expenses low and projecting an affordable yet sophisticated image, Euphoria is sure to become a leader in the massage therapy marketplace. As individuals continue to incur more stress in their daily lives, the need for "relaxing indulgences" such as Euphoria is sure to increase.

Euphoria
Relaxing Indulgences

DESCRIPTION OF VENTURE

People are always looking for solutions that will help them relax and enjoy themselves more. Euphoria plans to help people do this by offering comfortable and affordable massages and great skin care and aromatherapy products in a plush atmosphere. By offering a "menu of massages," customers will be able to easily identify with whatever relaxing indulgence they choose. Customers will visit just to browse our wide selection of skin care and aromatherapy products available for sale, to get a massage, or a combination of the two.

The inside of the store will have plush furniture where customers can wait before the massage and look at our wide range of skin care and aromatherapy products. These products will be visible from the street and will entice pedestrians to come inside. Euphoria plans to rent a small space that can be opened up with mirrors and other velvet drapes sectioning off the different areas where people will receive their massages. Traditional, off-white massage chairs will be covered in velvet material to make them fit in with the decor of the store. Euphoria plans to create a relaxing atmosphere where people can go for a brief escape from reality.

Looking for a new challenge? The Vault Job Board has thousands of top jobs for all experience levels. Visit www.vault.com.

VAULT CAREER LIBRARY **151**

DESCRIPTION OF VENTURE, CONT'D

New York City is the ideal place for the first store, because it is a trendy place where many people work in addition to those just wandering the streets shopping. There are several districts of Manhattan that host many fashionable restaurants, bars, and stores.

Stress continues to cause mental and health problems worldwide. As the number of hours people work continues to increase, stress rises in the workplace and in other areas. This will further necessitate the need for stress-relieving opportunities. For this reason, massages are being touted at one of the hottest business opportunities in the upcoming years by sources such as *Entrepreneur* magazine. Women have always had a love for skin care and aromatherapy products and men are becoming more interested now also. These products will serve as great window items to lure people into a store. Euphoria plans to offer an affordable way for people to relax in a very plush and cozy atmosphere where they can escape from the rest of the world.

Currently, the main competitors to Euphoria are The Great American Back Rub and various luxury spas located in New York. The Great American Back Rub offers traditional massages and other ergonomic products to its customers. The problem is that they have a medicinal décor and do not create an upscale and

Euphoria

Relaxing Indulgences

DESCRIPTION OF VENTURE, CONT'D

enticing image to attract customers. In addition, it costs almost $17 to receive a 10-minute massage. This goes beyond the normal price point that an individual is willing to pay for something relaxing on a regular basis. People are accustomed to paying close to $10 for a movie ticket or manicure, but having to pay $17 for a 10-minute massage makes it more of an extravagance than a normal weekly activity. By giving 15-minute massages for $15, we see our service as a more affordable way to attract a larger customer base. In addition, a 15-minute break from work, whether at lunch or after the day is done, is more of an indulgence than The Great American Back Rub's 10 minutes, yet requires less of a commitment than a long, expensive spa appointment. Euphoria will offer discounts on monthly packages to get customers in the habit of having a massage once a week or more. Euphoria is meant for everyone to enjoy, and for people to be able to afford on more of a regular basis.

Due to the fact that massage therapists must be licensed in certain states, such as New York, it is imperative to hire people who have attained the necessary licenses and want to be a part of a young and growing business venture. In addition, the main financial variable will be the cost and length of the lease obtained in the high rent districts of New York City. Euphoria will purchase its skin care and aromatherapy products from various manufacturers across the United States.

Looking for a new challenge? The Vault Job Board has thousands of top jobs for all experience levels. Visit www.vault.com.

VAULT CAREER LIBRARY **153**

Euphoria

Relaxing Indulgences

DESCRIPTION OF VENTURE, CONT'D

The secret of Euphoria is its ability to generate profits and revenues very quickly once initial expenses have been covered. After the initial expenses associated with opening the store are incurred, there are relatively few monthly expenses and almost every service offered produces 100 percent profit (minus rent and labor). In addition, the profit margins on skin care and aromatherapy items are very high, as long as inventory is kept to a minimum. There exist many other profitable opportunities for Euphoria, including hair, facial and body products, aromatherapy and skin care gifts, gift certificates, commercial in-store advertising, sales of fresh desserts and fruit drinks, and openings of additional stores in Manhattan, expansion to other major cities, commercial office buildings and upscale malls. Euphoria will profit because of the products and services offered and its ambitions to reproduce its winning formula for profitability in cities nationwide. Euphoria plans to use earnings from its first store, in addition to possible future rounds of financing, to open other stores in Manhattan and in other major cities nationwide. Long-term goals include possible franchising and a public stock offering.

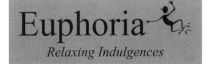

MERCHANDISING PLAN

Euphoria plans to purchase aromatherapy and skin care products from approximately seven to ten upscale manufacturers. We will offer a menu of different massages that customers can choose from. In addition, customers will be able to indulge in a dessert or fruit drink before or after their massage.

Massage Menu

The Euphoria Experience

Head and Neck Massage

Back Massage

Head, Neck and Back Massage

Arm and Hand Massage

Hand Massage

Foot Massage

Foot and Leg Massage

Back Scratch

Pressure Point Massage

Heating & Cooling Packs

$15

(approximately 15 minutes in length)

Looking for a new challenge? The Vault Job Board has thousands of top jobs for all experience levels. Visit www.vault.com.

VAULT CAREER LIBRARY

155

MERCHANDISING PLAN, CONT'D

Euphoria Aromatherapy

Aromatherapy Candles

Skin Lotions

Bath Gels

Heating and Cooling Packs

Massage Rollers

Euphoria Indulgence

Natural Fruit Juices/Shakes

Cakes and Pastries

Ice Creams and Sorbets

Euphoria

Relaxing Indulgences

MARKETING PLAN

Euphoria plans to market itself through advertising media such as online, print, billboards, and other techniques. We feel that creating the right image for Euphoria will be one of the keys to success. By creating a classy image that appeals to all types of individuals, Euphoria hopes to capture a diverse group of recurring customers.

Our marketing and advertising campaign will focus on three main points.

- An upscale and trendy environment that offers an escape from reality.
- Relaxing indulgences that help alleviate stress.
- An affordable way to relax that can be done on a regular basis.

Most individuals only visit spas once in a while, due to cost factors. By having affordable rates, Euphoria plans to become the affordable way to relieve stress on a regular basis. We plan to induce a whole new group of people to try massages who have not done so in the past.

Looking for a new challenge? The Vault Job Board has thousands
of top jobs for all experience levels. Visit www.vault.com.

VAULT CAREER LIBRARY   157

Euphoria
Relaxing Indulgences

MARKETING PLAN, CONT'D

Euphoria will place ads in publications such as *Time Out New York* and *The New Yorker*. We plan on placing ads on buses and in certain billboard locations. We will also have individuals handing out fliers near the store. We will work with corporations to offer special discounts to their employees. We hope to establish a relationship where they can link to our web site from their corporate services home page for employees make an appointment or send a gift certificate online. Euphoria plans to advertise using a variety of media to reach the diverse population of New York and appeal to all types of people.

Euphoria

Relaxing Indulgences

ORGANIZATIONAL PLAN

Current Plan

Jennifer Pirone

↓

Store Manager

↓

Massage Therapists

Future Plan

Jennifer Pirone

↓

V.P Advertising / Operations Manager / V.P. Expansion

↓

Store Managers

↓

Massage Therapists

Looking for a new challenge? The Vault Job Board has thousands
of top jobs for all experience levels. Visit www.vault.com.

VAULT CAREER LIBRARY   159

ASSESSMENT OF RISK

The risk associated with Euphoria is getting individuals accustomed to affordable massages on a regular basis. The massage marketplace is growing rapidly and Euphoria plans to capitalize on this by being the first business to the marketplace that projects the right type of image and services. The importance of store locations will also be a key part of Euphoria's success. Each location must be accessible to professionals, shoppers and other pedestrians. Euphoria will attempt to brand itself as the "cool" place to go for an inexpensive, yet very relaxing and enjoyable experience. Once we have established this, we are confident that individuals will come to Euphoria on a regular basis to receive massages and purchase aromatherapy and skin care products.

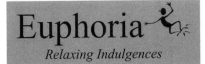

FINANCIAL PLAN

Projected Start-Up Costs

Projected Income Statement

Projected Statement of Cash Flows

Looking for a new challenge? The Vault Job Board has thousands
of top jobs for all experience levels. Visit www.vault.com.

VAULT CAREER LIBRARY **161**

Glossary

Accounts payable: A liability incurred by a company when it buys goods or services on credit or on account with a vendor.

Accounts receivable: Amounts owed by customers to a company when the company delivers goods or services on credit to those customers.

Angel: A (usually wealthy) person who provides cash in a start-up venture in exchange for equity in the venture. Angel investments are typically less formal and less restrictive than venture capital investments.

Assets: Economic resources owned by a company (e.g., cash, accounts receivable, computers, and inventory).

Balance sheet: A snapshot of a company's financial position at a specific point in time; in a balance sheet, assets always equal liabilities plus owners' equity.

Board of directors: The individuals who make up a corporation's board and set policy for the corporation to benefit stockholders.

Boiler plate: Parts of a contract that are standard or generic.

Burn rate: The rate at which a venture is spending (or "burning") cash

Capitalization: The total money (equity plus long-term debt) invested in a company.

Cash flow: Cash in minus cash out over a specific period (e.g., a fiscal quarter or year)

Cost of goods sold: Also known as COGS, this figure represents a company's costs of items sold for a particular accounting period (like a month); COGS for a specific period are always inventory at the beginning of the period plus purchases during the period, minus inventory left over at the end of the period

Current assets: Assets like cash, accounts receivable and other assets that the company expects will be converted into cash within one year.

Current liabilities: Liabilities like accounts payable, debts and other liabilities due within one year.

Depreciation: The amount of an asset's cost that is expensed in a specific period (like a month), to reflect that period's benefit from the use of the asset.

Dilution: A reduction in a shareholder's share in a company, usually when the company sells additional stock to new shareholders.

Dividends: Distributions of cash (or shares) to stockholders, usually to distribute some or all of the company's profits.

Downside: The amount of risk someone takes in a deal, including the possible loss of the entire investment.

Due diligence: The process of investigating a company prior to making an investment in it.

Equity: Also known as stock, owners' equity or shareholders' equity; the preferred or common stock of a business; also assets minus liabilities.

Executive summary: A summary of the contents of a company's business plan, usually one page.

Exit strategy: A company's strategy for turning the value of the business into cash or liquid stock. Usually the exit strategy involves "going public" in an IPO, or selling the company to another company.

"Go public": See "IPO."

IPO: An initial public offering; the process by which a company sells its stock to the general public for the first time, usually on a stock exchange.

Liabilities: Obligations, or amounts owed, by a company to vendors, lenders and the like.

Mezzanine financing: Money raised by a company that is expecting to "go public" in the near future.

Price-earnings ratio: Also called the P/E ratio; the ratio of the price of the company's stock to its earnings in the last 12 months. (For example, a company has a P/E of 20 if its stock trades at $100 a share and its profits equal $5 per share.)

Public offering: The sale of stock in a company to the general public, usually on a stock exchange.

Registration rights: Rights granted to an investor to register his stock in the company with the U.S. Securities and Exchange Commission (SEC) in order to sell them to the public.

Looking for a new challenge? The Vault Job Board has thousands
of top jobs for all experience levels. Visit www.vault.com.

VAULT CAREER LIBRARY   **163**

Retained income: Also called retained earnings; retained income represents the total shareholders' equity plus profits generated by a business, minus the dividends the company has paid.

Rolodex round: The first round of financing in a venture, including investments from founders, friends and family.

Stock options: Special rights granted to an individual or entity to purchase a corporation's stock at a set price (also called the exercise price) until a specific date (upon which the options are no longer exercisable).

Upside: The greatest amount of money someone can make by investing in a venture.

Valuation: The total monetary value of an entity.

Venture capitalist: A person or firm that provides cash in a high-risk venture in exchange for equity in the venture, with the expectation of earning a potentially high rate of return.

Vesting: Usually related to stock or stock options granted to a company's employees, conditioned on an employee's remaining with the company for some period of time; vesting is the process by which, over time, the employee earns the unconditional right to the stock or stock options.

Working capital: A company's current assets minus its current liabilities.

About the Author

Jonathan R. Aspatore has served as a consultant for various technology and retail companies, offering his expertise in entrepreneurial and equity research. He has worked in the Derivatives Products Group at Morgan Stanley in New York and for Wallace Willmore Cromwell & Co., a boutique investment bank with offices just outside of Washington, D.C. and San Francisco. Mr. Aspatore graduated from the University of Pennsylvania studying entrepreneurial management in the Wharton School of Business. He has founded two product companies, an entrepreneurial consulting firm, and is involved with numerous web sites devoted to the needs of small business owners and entrepreneurs.

Looking for a new challenge? The Vault Job Board has thousands of top jobs for all experience levels. Visit www.vault.com.

VAULT CAREER LIBRARY **165**